dedicated to my mom for
showing me the connection
between food, family and love

A Wealth of Insight:

*The World's Best Chefs on
Creativity, Leadership, and Perfection*

by Rahim B. Kanani

ISBN 978-1-63393-871-7

Published by

BLACK
TRUFFLE
PRESS

www.blacktruffleclub.com

Cover Photo Courtesy of Amber
Photo to the Right by Paulo Barata for Belcanto

About the Author

Rahim B. Kanani is a leadership, luxury, travel and dining contributor to a number of global publications, and has interviewed more than 600 of the world's foremost executives and innovators on leadership, management and creativity. His first book, *A Wealth of Insight: The World's Best Luxury Hoteliers on Leadership, Management, and the Future of 5-Star Hospitality (2018)*, was critically-acclaimed by leading hospitality schools and industry executives as required reading for current and aspiring luxury hotel managers. His second book, *A Wealth of Insight: The World's Best Chefs on Creativity, Leadership and Perfection (2019)*, profiles nearly 45 culinary icons who have collectively amassed nearly 100 Michelin stars, and who regularly appear atop the World's 50 Best Restaurants, La Liste, James Beard and other international rankings and awards.

Over the years, notable interviewees have included billionaires Jeff Skoll, Michael Bloomberg, Tory Burch and Eli Broad, world-renowned chefs Eric Ripert, Daniel Humm, José Andrés, and Anthony Bourdain, musical artists Alicia Keys, Madonna, and Shakira, Hollywood filmmaker James Cameron, Harvard University President Drew Faust, former British Prime Minister Tony Blair, and Princess Ameerah Al-Taweel of Saudi Arabia. During this time, Rahim served as a leadership contributor to *Forbes* and *Thomson Reuters Foundation*, while also authoring or editing articles and interviews published in *Harvard Business Review*, *CNN Opinion*, *Financial Times*, *Fast Company*, *Food & Wine* and others.

A native of Vancouver, Canada, Rahim resides in Washington, DC.

A Wealth of Insight

The World's Best Chefs on
Creativity, Leadership and Perfection

RAHIM B. KANANI

Table of Contents

Foreword by Ferran Adrià x

Introduction 1

Anthony Bourdain (1956—2018)
(New York, NY, USA) 5

Aaron Silverman—Pineapple and Pearls
(Washington, DC, USA) 8

Albert Adrià—Tickets
(Barcelona, Spain) 12

Alex Atala—D.O.M.
(São Paulo, Brazil). 16

Ana Roš—Hiša Franko
(Kobarid, Slovenia) 20

Andoni Luis Aduriz—Mugaritz
(San Sebastián, Spain) 24

Chan Yan Tak—Lung King Heen
(Hong Kong) 30

Cristina Bowerman—Glass Hostaria
(Rome, Italy) 36

David Kinch—Manresa
(Los Gatos, CA, USA) 40

Emma Bengtsson—Aquavit
(New York, NY, USA) 44

Emmanuel Stroobant—Shoukouwa
(Singapore) 50

Eneko Azurmendi—Azurmendi
(Larrabetzu, Spain) 56

Enrico Crippa—Piazza Duomo
(Alba, Italy) 60

Éric Frechon—Epicure
(Paris, France) 64

Eric Ripert—Le Bernardin
(New York, NY, USA) 68

**Georgianna Hiliadaki and
Nikos Roussos**—Funky Gourmet
(Athens, Greece). 74

Guillaume Galliot—Caprice
(Hong Kong) 78

Guy Savoy—Guy Savoy
(Paris, France) 82

Hans Neuner—Ocean
(Algarve, Portugal) 86

Jacob Jan Boerma—De Leest
(Vaassen, The Netherlands) 90

Joachim Wissler—Vendôme
(Bergisch Gladbach, Germany) 94

Joan Roca—El Celler de Can Roca
(Girona, Spain) 98

Jonnie Boer—De Librije
(Zwolle, The Netherlands). 102

José Andrés—minibar
(Washington, DC, USA) 108

José Avillez—Belcanto
(Lisbon, Portugal) 112

Kevin Fehling—The Table
(Hamburg, Germany). 118

Kwong Wai Keung—T'ang Court
(Hong Kong) 124

Martha Ortiz—Dulce Patria
(Mexico City, Mexico) 128

Martin Berasategui—Martin Berasategui
(Lasarte-Oria, Spain) 132

Matthew Orlando—Amass
(Copenhagen, Denmark) 138

Nicolai Nørregaard—Kadeau
(Copenhagen, Denmark) 144

Niki Nakayama—n/naka
(Los Angeles, CA, USA) 150

Patrick O'Connell—The Inn at Little
Washington (Washington, VA, USA) . .154

Pedro Subijana—Akelarre
(San Sebastián, Spain) 160

Peter Goossens—Hof van Cleve
(Kruishoutem, Belgium) 164

Ricardo Costa—The Yeatman
(Porto, Portugal) 168

Richard Ekkebus—Amber
(Hong Kong) 174

Rodolfo Guzmán—Boragó
(Santiago, Chile) 180

Ryuki Kawasaki—Mezzaluna
(Bangkok, Thailand) 186

Sean Gray—Ko
(New York, NY, USA) 190

Sven Elverfeld—Aqua
(Wolfsburg, Germany) 196

Tetsuya Wakuda—Waku Ghin
(Singapore) 200

Virgilio Martínez—Central
(Lima, Peru) 206

Foreword

Photo by Juancho Everman

f I tried to identify the most important element of *avant-garde* cuisine of the past twenty years, I have no doubt that it would be the search for creativity—a radical, absolute search. By contrast, in the 20th century, the objective was not so much to innovate, but to reach perfection inside parameters that did not change. For in the era of great classical cuisine, the public expected to taste dishes they already knew.

In other periods, such as the era of *nouvelle cuisine,* people tended to question this heritage. Chefs from this period carved a path for personal innovation, authorship, affirmation of individual style, and questioning truths that have been taken for granted during the golden age of classical cuisine.

A disruptive step was taken in the middle of the nineties: an incorruptible search for creativity at all costs, and the standardization of this creativity. During this decade at elBulli, we not only had to invent recipes, but we also had to try to build a methodology, a philosophy, an infrastructure, and a series of resources that would allow us to innovate continuously and deeply.

In 1994, we began "technical-conceptual creativity"—the search for generic techniques and concepts that give birth to all kinds of creations and dishes. In 1995, we became aware of another fundamental idea: we could play with ingredients beyond the purely physical by adding provocation, surprise, irony, decontextualization, childhood memories and more. We were turning the act of eating into a global experience that stimulated the mind, emotions, and sensorial perception. At the end of the nineties, we established the first workshop in the world dedicated to researching *haute cuisine*. The sum of these moments helped define the direction of contemporary cuisine.

Circling around the kitchens of the best restaurants in the world is enough to realize that the seed planted at elBulli, and other places in Spain and around the world, continues to bear fruit.

Rahim Kanani analyzes and illustrates this reality in *A Wealth of Insight* which, for the first time, comprehensively addresses creativity in contemporary cuisine without neglecting its roots. In an authentic panorama covering every corner of the world, Kanani documents all the innovation systems developed in the workshops and kitchens of the most outstanding chefs of the moment, ranging from the most holistic approach to the purely artistic. His vision is a loyal reflection of contemporary cuisine, allowing us to approach an unquestionable truth: there has never in history been a richer, more prepared, more diverse, and more stimulating generation of chefs pushing culinary boundaries than there are today. This reality cannot make me prouder.

I hope you appreciate and enjoy *A Wealth of Insight* as much as I do, for these pages constitute a true world atlas of creativity and innovation of the 21st century kitchen.

Chef Ferran Adrià

Introduction

The idea for this book, unbeknownst to me at the time, originated in November 2012 during an hours-long tasting menu of pure discovery at minibar by Chef José Andrés in Washington DC. It was my first experience at a restaurant designed and built for gastronomes, and one that was revered worldwide for its creativity and innovation. Course after course was awe-inspiring, imaginative and superb. Witnessing the culinary freedom, precision and thoughtfulness that embodied the minibar experience was like awakening my palette from a coma. I walked away with a sense of wonder and curiosity not just about the world of cuisine, but about life.

Growing up, I was the only child of three who was naturally drawn to helping our mother in the kitchen cook everything from roti, an Indian flatbread stroked with butter while hot, to vegetable curry made with potatoes and peas, to biryani, a highly fragrant dish of marinated meat, ground spices, caramelized onions and fluffy saffron rice. Like virtually every chef profiled in this book, I was inspired to love food and the art of cooking by serving as a helping hand to mom. And like all great motherly cuisine, there were no recipes, only decades of experience punctuated by instinct. Indeed, I lost count of how many times a chef would reference their favorite dish as something their mother or grandmother used to make. That

nostalgia, they said, was intimately tied to childhood memories of gathering around the kitchen table, connecting, sharing, laughing and smiling with family and friends. In essence, food was at the center of love.

For more than six years following minibar, I immersed myself in a personal quest to better understand and experience five-star cuisine and culinary genius by dining at some of the finest restaurants in the world. I became obsessed with a chef's creative process, their ability to constantly reinterpret cuisine, their unrelenting pursuit of perfection, and their unwavering commitment to excellence. Now, after a year of digging deeper into the minds of nearly 45 of the world's best chefs who have collectively amassed nearly 100 Michelin stars, and who are regularly featured atop the World's 50 Best Restaurants, La Liste, James Beard and other international rankings and awards, I am honored and humbled to share the fruits of that labor.

If you are endlessly fascinated by how the world's best chefs get inspired, create and innovate, research critically-acclaimed restaurateurs and food reviews months before taking a trip, are addicted to TV shows and documentaries that showcase food culture, cuisine and culinary personalities from all over the world, or secretly dream of crisscrossing continents as an insatiable gastrotourist, then *A*

Wealth of Insight is for you. In addition, for those eager to learn how these five-star chefs began their journey to the top and maintain their prime position, this book also dives into their childhood memories, early experiences, culinary philosophy, how best to lead and manage a world-class restaurant, the future of food and their advice to young and aspiring chefs.

Pulling back the curtain on the creative process reveals a web of wisdom not only about the world of cuisine, but also about human ingenuity more generally. Like a musician who composes a piece of music entirely in their mind before ever writing a score, or an artist who visualizes a painting before ever putting pencil to paper, or a perfumer who imagines a particular aroma before setting out to create it, culinary creativity begins in the brain. One of the most profound insights to emerge from this endeavor was that those profiled in the book are able to mix and match flavors and textures entirely in their minds—intellectually tasting combinations that have yet to exist. They rely solely on an encyclopedic memory of flavor profiles and an instinct honed over decades of pairing ingredients from all over the world in every season. This alone is an astonishing ability.

Another insightful discovery was how every chef exhibited a deep philosophical and holistic understanding of food, nature and the art of cooking. Food brought friends and family together, evoked memories and emotions, nourished and healed the mind and body, captivated all five senses, and conveyed a story of history, art, seasonality and humanity. A plate of food was a plate of life. I quickly realized that these particular chefs brought a level of academic rigor, honesty, authenticity and soul to their pursuits akin to the great philosophers and truth-seekers of our time. While there was no consensus among these chefs on whether creativity could be taught or whether it was innate, they all believed that it could not flourish in the dark.

Every chef was adamant that creativity must be grounded in a fundamental understanding and experience of the past—flavors, combinations and techniques. Without a mastery of tradition, they argued, there is no benchmark, and without a benchmark, there is no foundation from which to evolve and elevate. In other words, creativity is fueled by experience, coupled with a natural curiosity about the world and an openness to being inspired.

As with all experimentation, there are inevitable setbacks—too many to count—but these instances are not seen as failures. They are embraced as opportunities to refine, test and perfect a dish. It is part and parcel of the creative process, and every chef profiled relishes that intentional and improvisational effort, rather than considering it a burden. Accepting this amount of trial and error requires perseverance, discipline and an investigative mentality, not unlike a detective, to follow every new lead and gut instinct wherever they may lead. On rare occasions, a dish will translate perfectly from mind to plate, taking a few days to appear on the menu. More often than not, however, the process can take weeks, months, and even years to reach a level where these chefs feel comfortable serving it to their diners.

As it turns out, the spark of inspiration is ignited most often outside the kitchen: perusing the local market, traveling near or far, reading a book of fiction, listening to music, walking through the woods, riding a bike or while simply taking a shower. Other times, a spark is lit spontaneously, for one chef explained that there was nothing more inspiring than 5kg of chanterelle mushrooms, picked 30 minutes ago, coming through the backdoor in the middle of service.

Another surprising nugget to surface across interviews was that nearly every chef profiled carries a notebook, wherever they are in the world, to document their ideas and inspirations in real-time—habitually and obsessively. They write down new flavor combinations that spring to mind, new ingredients just discovered, new cooking techniques just witnessed, emotions they wish to trigger, or something as brief as the hint of a passing aroma.

When creating a new dish, many chefs explained that before they step foot into a kitchen and begin experimenting, they visualize the product on paper in great detail, drawing a fully plated dish—mimicking the sketch of an architect. This is because the intellectual work of a new dish comes first. What product are we trying to showcase? What method should we use to cook it? What flavors and textures complement the star ingredient? What order should the dish be eaten and therefore, how should it be plated? And finally, in what vessel should it be served?

Only until recently did the culinary profession garner the kind of cultish respect, admiration and reverence that it commands today. The most talented of people who could succeed at any number of careers, several chefs excitedly pointed out, are now choosing to become a cook. Back then, the profession was pursued as a sheer passion and as a means to earn a living. One did not always follow the other, and only those who were determined, passionate and resilient flourished. Capturing that juxtaposition and staying power, a number of chefs profiled in *A Wealth of Insight* have been cooking for more than four decades.

Throughout history, chefs have been stewards of not only culinary tradition, but also of cultural heritage, intellectual freedom, creative spirit and masterful manual labor. In short, respecting and cherishing their place in society is long overdue, and we owe them a great deal.

Finally, as a tribute, I begin this book with an abridged interview I conducted with the late Anthony Bourdain on relentlessly pursuing your passion without regard to what the world thinks. Chef Bourdain was one of the most vibrant, eye-opening and fearless culinary explorers to have ever lived, and someone who inspired millions like myself to never let the torch of curiosity and thirst for knowledge fade into the night.

The search for wisdom continues.

Rahim B. Kanani
rahim@rahimkanani.com

Anthony Bourdain

NEW YORK, NY, USA

(1956 – 2018)

"**This profession has always been accepting of all kinds of people—refugees, maniacs and misfits—but to excel at it, only the few, the proud, and the weird will flourish.**"

FULL OF SURPRISES

Travel, like anything in life, cannot be boiled down to a couple of sweeping statements. It's all gray. That's why I do it. I love going to a little place and thinking I know something about it and being completely surprised. Even if it's embarrassing, painful and awkward, and I look like an idiot. Knowledge is not bad.

I AM GRATEFUL

I have seen first-hand that things can turn on a dime. Tremendously awful, evil things happen to nice people all the time. I have seen people, again and again, relentlessly grinding under the wheel of poverty or oppression. At the same time, I see random acts of kindness and pride in the most outrageous and most unexpected circumstances. I am grateful. I understand that I am very privileged to see what I'm seeing, even when it hurts. I think that people, particularly Americans, need to be more inspired to travel and be adventurous with the things they eat. And if they are curious about the world and willing to walk in somebody else's shoes, that is surely a good thing.

AN EARLY LESSON

I never, ever, ever think about my success. That's the road to madness, egomania and mediocrity. When you start thinking about what people like, you start thinking about what people expect. Then you start pandering to people's expectations. I learned very early on not to think about that. You go out there and do the best you can. You do things that are interesting to you, and hopefully they'll be interesting to other people too. I don't want to be adequate. I'd rather fail gloriously making something strange and awesome, but ultimately a failure.

NOTHING MORE POLITICAL

Why do people cook what they cook? Who eats? Who doesn't? There's nothing more political than food. It is always the end or a part of a long story, often a painful one. I travel around the world asking people what makes them happy, what do they eat and what would they like their kids to eat ten years from now, and I get some really interesting and complicated answers in places like Beirut, Iran, Vietnam, and even Detroit.

THE REALITY OF THIS BUSINESS

Let's face it, if you're rolling out of culinary school and your highest aspiration is to be on TV, or you think you're ready to make the big bucks, good luck with that because your prospects are not good. No matter what people see on TV, at the end of the day, the antibodies of the restaurant business will push out the pretenders and only the strong will survive. The people with vision and determination, as throughout history, are the people that last. This profession has always been accepting of all kinds of people—refugees, maniacs and misfits—but to excel at it, only the few, the proud, and the weird will flourish.

⁂

This abridged interview with the late Anthony Bourdain was conducted in January 2016. Chef Bourdain was one of the most vibrant, eye-opening and fearless culinary explorers to have ever lived, and someone who inspired millions like myself to never let the torch of curiosity and thirst for knowledge fade into the night. His legacy will forever live in each of us.

Aaron Silverman

BORN IN:

Silver Spring, MD, USA

BASED IN:

Washington, DC, USA

EXPERIENCE:

13 years

SELECT ACCOLADES:

Pineapple and Pearls | 87.00/100 in La Liste (2019)

Pineapple and Pearls | 2 Michelin Stars (2019)

Rose's Luxury | 1 Michelin Star (2019)

Photo to the Left by Kate Warren
All Other Photos by Anna Meyer

"The willingness to let failures take you in a different direction and guide you to success is the essence of creativity. "

THE MOMENT

While cooking at home with my father when I was young helped build an interest in cooking, the key moment that led me on this journey was a month long stage at 2941 Restaurant in Falls Church, Virginia, while I was on winter break in college. I torched tomatoes, picked herbs from their garden and learned to slice smoked salmon, and after the experience I was so excited about cooking that I finished college a year early just to enroll in culinary school.

A TEACHING KITCHEN

The first kitchen I worked in was, still to this day, the toughest and most challenging kitchen I have ever worked in as a cook. The days were unbelievably long with absolutely no breaks or moments to catch your breath. At the same time, it was incredibly enjoyable and rewarding, as it was an extremely high-performance kitchen and nothing short of perfect was accepted. Many would call this a "teaching kitchen" because while the chefs demanded perfection, they also spent a lot of time teaching us new skills and techniques.

KNOWING THE DIFFERENCE

The most important leadership lesson I've learned is understanding the difference between a manager and a leader. A manager completes tasks, while a leader inspires, motivates, challenges and rewards his or her team. In order to be a great chef, you must be both a great manager and a great leader.

COMMUNICATION IS CRITICAL

The best way to build a world-class team is to encourage strong communication amongst all colleagues, and the best way to retain that team is to continuously challenge and reward them. I would describe our leadership style as communicative, supportive and inclusive of a high-performance culture.

LIVING UP TO THE HYPE

One of the challenges for us is living up to the hype and expectations of our restaurants. We have been lucky enough to garner a lot of positive press over the years, and dealing with that pressure can be tough. Remaining humble and focused on our mission helps us stay grounded and calm.

TASTE EVERY DISH

Maintaining consistency is very difficult in any restaurant but especially when the bar is set so high. Extreme attention to detail and a strong system of supervision and quality control are how we maintain consistency. For instance, at each restaurant we taste every single dish every single day in its entirety before service starts—to make sure everything is spot on.

WE HAVE A RESPONSIBILITY

The biggest challenge for us is keeping everyone motivated, inspired and happy. The happiness of my staff, from top to bottom, is what keeps me up at night. The whole reason I decided to open up my own restaurant was to make people happy—not just guests but staff as well. I spend countless hours considering what more we can do for our staff to ensure everyone is taken care of. The best thing we offer is an inclusive, enjoyable and positive work environment, and a solid benefits package that includes health, dental, parental leave and paid time off. As restaurant operators and chefs, we have a responsibility to take care of our staff and ourselves, and to promote good health and wellbeing. Many think this is not possible due to the historically slim margins of restaurants, but as a restaurant group, we want to prove otherwise.

WILLING TO FAIL

The willingness to let failures take you in a different direction and guide you to success is the essence of creativity. When we receive criticism, face setbacks, or get a bad review, we choose to use those

instances as learning tools and opportunities to improve. Everyone gets knocked down once in a while. That's normal. That's not failure. Failure is when you refuse to get back up and try again.

COCONUT AND CAVAIR

The creative process involves a lot of tinkering, trial and error. Some of our most bizarre ideas have helped foster the most successful dishes. One example of this is when I was working with our chef de cuisine at Rose's Luxury. We were playing with the idea of a savory **île** *flottante*, which included *uni* and mustard. After multiple iterations that we were not satisfied with, we decided to try adding coconut and caviar to the dish. After tasting it all together, we were still not satisfied. However, we realized how incredible the coconut and caviar

tasted together so we decided to serve a scoop of coconut sorbet topped with white sturgeon caviar inside of a coconut shell instead. We scrapped the whole *île flottante* idea. This new combination became an instant hit and is now a signature dish.

EYES OF THE BEHOLDER

There is such a thing as a perfect dish, but it lies in the eyes of the beholder. Imperfections are much more interesting encounters to me than the idea of perfection. I also love balancing tradition with new techniques as it creates excitement when you contrast the two. At Rose's Luxury, for example, we sometimes serve a classic *cacio e pepe* on the menu. I could never imagine adding basil or ricotta to the dish, but what's the fun of life if you don't innovate and experiment?

Albert Adrià

BORN IN:

Barcelona, Spain

BASED IN:

Barcelona, Spain

EXPERIENCE:

33 years

SELECT ACCOLADES:

Tickets | 1 Michelin Star (2019)

Tickets | No. 32 on the World's 50 Best (2018)

Enigma | 1 Michelin Star (2019)

Photos by Moisés Torné

"The creative process is not very methodical. Seldom is a plate formed and finished in its first phase."

AN UNLIKELY CAREER

As a kid, I didn't have any particular interest in cuisine. When I was 15 years old, I entered elBulli because my brother Ferran was the head chef and he needed cooks. I never dreamed of becoming a chef. I had no idea what cooking was or what being a cook entailed. My passion for cuisine started to grow from that moment on. It became a lifestyle because we worked, ate and slept in the restaurant. For two years I moved from station to station, learning everything I could. I finally ended up in baking, and there I stayed because I was drawn to the level of knowledge and technique that were required to be a good baker.

ANXIETY AND EXCELLENCE

I understand that I'm still young and have much to say, but it is important to embrace newer generations in this industry and grow old with dignity. The fact that I have lived for so many years isolated at elBulli makes me a confident person, but the key is to stay as pure as possible in your approach and philosophy in order to avoid the anxiety and stress that comes with wider recognition.

THE KEYS TO SUCCESS

Nothing keeps me awake at night. I sleep perfectly. I work a lot, but as I've gotten older, I've learned to relax and enjoy the things I've accomplished—much of which I never imagined. Passion and humbleness are the keys to success. For me, passion is working 15-hour days and humbleness is waking up thinking you know nothing. Those two things are enough for me. In the end, to cook is an exercise of common sense mixed with some bravery.

CONSTANT CRITICISM

When I first received a bad review or was criticized in some way, I used to react with nervousness, but now the criticism itself, and the frequency of that criticism has changed. Today, you are constantly the focus of attention on social media. Not a day goes by when you are not criticized, complimented or even insulted. This routine has created an indifference in my reaction.

FUELING CREATIVITY

There are routines and lessons that you can put into practice and teach so that someone has a creative attitude, but in the end, a creative person is driven by curiosity, which I think in many cases is innate. A creative attitude is not enough, though, to succeed. You need money to buy equipment, time, and a workspace to create. Experiments are necessary to make mistakes, and that is the key lesson. You don't experiment with customers. The feeling of success when being creative is a little tumultuous because there is no goal in mind. Maximum excitement is tied to a blank slate, and creativity is tied to emptiness.

MIND TO PLATE

The creative process is not very methodical. Seldom is a plate formed and finished in its first phase, when ideas are gathered from many sources. I compare this process to assembling a car. The most important piece is the chassis, and then you assemble the engine, axis, wheels, doors, windows and other parts, but it's not as systematic a process as it may seem. Moments of creation vary widely.

Sometimes we will work on a product, such as asparagus, before it's in season, creating plates for all of our restaurants. We keep these ideas at the ready as soon as asparagus season arrives with the best quality and price.

EVERYTHING EVOLVES

Perfection does not exist. It is true that some dishes come close to perfection, but I don't believe in closed plates that don't evolve, because everything in this world evolves, even if that evolution is sometimes imperceptible. Every year I review my recipes and dishes, offering a different vision. For example, in baking you search for more freshness, less fat and less sugar, as well as other nuances. Today, the search for healthier cooking is not limited to baking.

THE FUTURE OF FOOD

Nowadays, one doesn't go out and eat to get stuffed. There is a global movement towards more healthier cuisine with less fat, less sugar, and less quantity. In terms of our daily diets, we must find both equilibrium and variety. It is ironic that while we now have

hundreds of products at our disposal, we are reducing the number of products we eat. But if we don't do this, our society will be filled with people who have cardiovascular issues from a very young age. We also need to pay more attention to how much food is thrown out everyday around the world, and the amount of trash we as restaurants make.

to learn, not to mention the incredible variety of products we use every day from seafood to meat to vegetables. Learning traditional cuisine from your home country, coupled with other specialties like French cuisine, require more and more hours of practice each day. In the end, the more knowledge you have, the easier it will be to create new recipes.

KNOWLEDGE IS POWER

I would advise future chefs to not waste time. This is a profession with many truths and ways of understanding. We do not live to be 300 years old. And as soon as you become head chef, your learning slows down. There are many types of cuisine from around the world that take a very long time

15

Alex Atala

BORN IN:

São Paulo, Brazil

BASED IN:

São Paulo, Brazil

EXPERIENCE:

30 years

SELECT ACCOLADES:

D.O.M. | 95.25/100 in La Liste (2019)

D.O.M. | No. 30 on the World's 50 Best (2018)

D.O.M. | 2 Michelin Stars (2018)

Photo to the Left by Rubens Kato
All Other Photos by Ricardo D'Angelo

"Creativity flourishes from a solid foundation of knowledge. Any chef that wants to create a new recipe needs to have a strong understanding of classic cuisine."

A JOURNEY UNPLANNED

My training in Europe was the result of a traveling circumstance. When I first entered the kitchen, I never thought I would spend the rest of my life there. Today, we have great chefs all around the world and it's no longer mandatory for a young chef to go to Europe in order to acquire a certain level of skill. It might be good for the ego to see a "graduated in Europe" on your résumé, but that's not what drives me or the people who work with me. We are driven by a belief in our own purpose and it is rewarding to be recognized while doing it.

INFINITE POSSIBILITIES

After 30 years of working in the kitchen, what excites me the most, and what I've learned the most, is that this profession is an endless road and there are infinite possibilities. Putting my uniform on every morning makes me realize that the possibilities of my profession are far, far broader than I ever imagined. The journey does not slow down or stop, not even when you're awarded a Michelin star or secure a spot on the World's 50 Best Restaurants list.

BECOMING AN ENTREPRENEUR

Brazil is quite hostile to entrepreneurship and that's one of the biggest challenges to starting a restaurant, or any other business for that matter. Understanding the legalities of launching your own business can be quite complex and off-putting, and this lack of knowledge is a challenge for any chef who wishes to open their own restaurant. I knew very little about the process, and it was a challenging uphill battle to get it right.

SOCIAL TRANSFORMATION

Creativity by itself doesn't make much sense. It needs purpose, and the key to creativity is biodiversity. When spoken, biodiversity has no value, but when tasted, it gains value. That's a lesson that the slow food movement left for the world and something we are finally understanding here in Brazil. The food chain is a powerful tool for social transformation and for the safekeeping of biodiversity itself. We, as citizens, can definitely be a starting point towards more conscious consuming—one that is more in line with our ethics.

STAYING TRUE

I'm a tattooed man. I'm Brazilian. That is who I am. If I'm different, then I will be different. I might not be able to cook a French dinner as well as a French chef due to cultural reasons, but, following that logic, no one will offer a better Brazilian experience than me. The cuisine, the ingredients, the Brazilian flavors—I've known them since childhood. I believe in them, and that's what kicked off the whole D.O.M. Group.

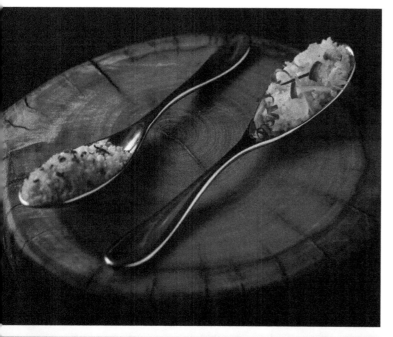

INSPIRING INGREDIENTS

Discovering a new flavor always encourages me to be creative and create something new, something that explores that flavor further and elevates our appreciation. Creativity doesn't exactly mean doing what nobody does. It means doing what everybody can do in a way nobody expects. We practice a products cuisine and deal with new ingredients every day. That's one of the major advantages of working with tasting menus.

TRICK QUESTION

If we ask ten people what good eating is, we will probably get ten different answers. However, if we ask the same ten people what bad eating is, we will probably come to a common understanding. With that in mind, it becomes possible to trace a path to the answer of whether or not the perfect dish exists. I don't think people need to be taught how to cook, act or eat. I do believe, however, that people should act more according to their personal ethics. Don't buy or eat something you don't agree with. This act generates a new demand and the market adjusts to it.

UNTIL THE DAY I DIE

When I first started, in the late 80s, I could never imagine that my job would allow me to be on TV or on the cover of magazines such as TIME. Back in those days, being a cook wasn't a cool job, especially in Brazil. We would take off the chef jacket to go shopping. It wasn't polite to show up in places wearing your work uniform. Today, you go to the mall and people are wearing it! It's a confirmation that being a chef has become an admired profes-

sion. Today, chefs are public figures with respected voices, as the advertisers of the 80s or the supermodels of the 90s. You put the chef jacket on and suddenly you gain superpowers. This is what I want to do until the day I die.

THE BEST WAY TO GROW

The best advice I could give to young chefs is that you must embody a spirit to overcome, not to settle, and to never believe what you've done is enough. You must be humble, too. I'm never ashamed to ask another chef to teach me. And how flattered I am when someone asks me, "Alex, how did you do that?" That's the best way to grow.

A FOUNDATION OF KNOWLEDGE

Traditional cooking, that "grandma spice," is absolutely essential to my cooking and to any professional working with haute cuisine. The main difference between good, very good and excellent dishes is the repetition. The more you do it, the better you get. In the world of cooking, creativity flourishes from a solid foundation of knowledge. A chef that wants to create new recipes needs to have a strong understanding of classic cuisine, which is rooted in traditional grandma spices. With that base of knowledge, the chef can create, bring new ingredients to the table, and think of new combinations. Without that base level of understanding, a chef cannot create with purpose.

Ana Roš

BORN IN:

Šempeter pri Gorici, Slovenia

BASED IN:

Kobarid, Slovenia

EXPERIENCE:

14 years

SELECT ACCOLADES:

Hiša Franko | 81.75/100 in La Liste (2019)

Hiša Franko | No. 48 on the World's 50 Best (2018)

Hiša Franko | Voted World's Best Female Chef (2017)

"You dream about perfection and are always on the hunt, but you curse the day you find it because this is the day you must stop cooking."

DISCOVERING A PASSION

Both of my grandmothers were great cooks. One was classical while the other was more creative and sophisticated. My mother too was a great cook, but as a journalist she never had time to bake or prepare lengthy meals. I myself never planned on becoming a cook. I was planning to pursue a diplomatic career and was about to take my first job in Brussels, but I fell in love with my husband who had a simple restaurant—Hiša Franko. Cooking in our society is considered a manual and unintellectual job, so I never had any support in my decision.

NEVER TOO LATE

I never trained in any professional kitchen. I am completely self-taught. I started cooking when I was 30 years old and pregnant for the first time. The next ten years were the hardest of my life. Every single day was a new discovery.

WORK-LIFE BALANCE

Cooking is a team effort, and our team is our family. Even my children understand that our chefs are one of us. We take care of each other and have fostered a real sense of work-life balance for our staff. Working in a kitchen is not necessarily just for young people. It should be lifelong work. We organize common activities including sports, running and yoga, and we serve two family meals every single day. Each meal is cooked by a different chef, and because our team is so international, we eat very diverse meals and learn about each other's culture. It is a holistic approach to how we treat, respect and care for our team.

THE RIGHT FEEDBACK

Hiša Franko is a countryside restaurant and we want to maintain that laidback atmosphere. For us to grow, I prefer to listen to positive criticism—and not destructive criticism—rather than nonstop congratulations. This is genuinely the only way to become better.

WE ARE STORYTELLERS

I am a dancer and a skier, both of which require discipline. Dancing, particularly the moments of improvisation, is intimately connected to creativity, which applies to the kitchen as well. If you are not creative, discipline alone won't help you become a great or interesting chef. You need to experiment with technique. That's what helps you advance. In the end, I believe we cook from our mind and soul: the hands just follow. We are storytellers, and storytellers need to have a lot of imagination.

SOURCES OF INSPIRATION

In addition to gathering ideas for new dishes, processes and techniques from my team, I am inspired by the world around me. Sometimes it can be a little moment of observing nature, listening to birds, or even dreaming. I always carry a notebook with me to jot down ideas, and when I find a new product in season, I start playing around with it. We discuss and develop these ideas as a team and elaborate on the core concept until we decide on the right dish.

THE POWER OF IMPERFECTION

You dream about perfection and are always on the hunt, but you curse the day you find it because this is the day you must stop cooking. Imperfection is the engine for evolution. I do not believe there are signature dishes that should never be changed or modified. Evolution, as the rest of nature and the world, is unstoppable and we must always adapt to change.

ECONOMIC AND SOCIAL IMPACT

Hiša Franko is so far away from the main cities that big suppliers could never reach us, so we needed to look to our surrounding. The locals were not very ambitious and were content with what they had. It took us a decade to convince them to share their products with us, and it took us 14 years to build a chain of more than 100 local producers and farmers to guarantee Hiša Franko would have the best quality products and produce.

This has had a huge economic and social impact for those living in Soča Valley. People garden for us, forage for us, farm for us, and we never question their price. Our products are the freshest and of the highest quality, having never travelled to another destination. You will not find these products anywhere else. It's a win-win situation. There is also a social impact to our work. Young people who tended to leave the valley because there were few jobs are now deciding to stay, having discovered opportunities to contribute. Traditional farming, milking, and gardening will not be forgotten, and this is something Hiša Franko is very proud of.

Andoni Luis Aduriz

BORN IN:

Errenteria, Spain

BASED IN:

San Sebastián, Spain

EXPERIENCE:

20 years

SELECT ACCOLADES:

Mugaritz | 83.75/100 in La Liste (2019)

Mugaritz | 2 Michelin Stars (2019)

Mugaritz | No. 9 on the World's 50 Best (2018)

Photo to the Left by Alex Iturralde
All Other Photos by José Luis López de Zubiria

> **"When you are trained to discover beauty, you can find beauty in everything. Creativity, therefore, is an attitude by which you discover."**

NEVER WITHOUT FOOD

I was a very bad student in secondary school. When I finished at 14 years old, I had no vocation in sight. My mother was very worried about my future, knowing I could follow the wrong path. She lived during the Spanish Civil War and suffered hunger and hardship. She wanted to be sure that I had enough to eat every day so she enrolled me in culinary school to become a chef.

HOW AM I GOING TO SURVIVE?

My earliest experiences in the kitchen were rather traumatic. I was 14 years old and, at the time, had only worked in simple restaurants and hotels. Seared in my memory is the always angry, dirty curmudgeon chef that was perpetually cruel. The first thing I thought was how am I going to survive? I was very ineffective. I used to run away because the chef, due to his weight and age, could not catch me.

BECOMING A LEADER

You can have a perfect command of language and speak very well, but if your actions do not align with your words, you are incoherent. This is not always the case, as sometimes your words express one thing and your actions express another, but when this happens, you will be remembered for your actions. You must understand this fact in order to become a leader.

CREATING A POSITIVE ECOSYSTEM

My time at elBulli coincided with the Balkan Wars after WWII. Apart from the ongoing atrocities, it was a war that we could empathize with because it was happening to people like us. All of this made me think that, logically, inside each of us resides the best and the worst. We are capable of both good and bad. If the context is appropriate to use all of our skills and creativity to inflict damage, then those skills would be activated as such. I came to

the conclusion that we needed to create an eco-system or an appropriate context in which all the skills and virtues of our team would blossom. I have since devoted myself to creating an environment that encourages creativity, loyalty and companion-ship in each person.

MEASURING SUCCESS

The success of Mugaritz must be measured against itself. We have the challenge of being true to the legacy. It's not easy to work for 20 years in a highly competitive environment with limited resources, and be considered one of the top ten restaurants in the world for the past 13 years. Places like Mug-aritz are a kind of high-performance center, where there are no limits to rigor. The job is incredibly de-manding. The key is not to be led astray by awards, compliments or critics.

CREATIVITY AS A BRIDGE

Gastronomy, generally speaking, is knowledge that has been sedimenting over time. Any dish viewed in the context of history will give us clues about the depth of the relationship humans have had with food. For instance, the seemingly simple relation-ship between human and tomato will surprise us because there was an original intent to create a product, underpinned by technology, desire and culture. Gastronomy needs many explanations to understand this complex relationship, and creativi-ty can serve as a bridge to uniquely explain, manage and convey that connection.

INSPIRE ME

Inspiration can come from a word, a gesture, a glance, an emotion, a technique or an ingredient. When you are trained to discover beauty, you can find beauty in everything. Creativity, therefore, is an attitude by which you discover. For example, lightness or decline are words that can serve as inspirations. In Mugaritz, we made a dish which evoked decline. The idea came from a picture: a scene that reflected 16th century Venice.

THE PERFECTION VACUUM

If you were to ask what the perfect meal was, my mind would immediately move to recreating, to some extent, what I already know and what belongs to my culture. Perfection is relative to the person. It does not exist in a vacuum.

THE REALITY OF CHANGE

Jacques Cousteau used to say that a tradition, in order to be a tradition, must adapt to new times. It is very difficult to find static traditions. In gas-tronomy, diasporas are often guardians of tradition because food serves as a unique reference to the origins people want to defend. Gastronomy, more generally, is constantly changing. It is not a good nor bad thing. It is just reality. Tradition has its place and we must respect it, but I work in the field of creativity. For me, tradition serves as a useful reference, but my profession is meant to ignore it.

mugaritz

A CURIOUS DISH

One way to create a new dish is from the perspective of curiosity. I enjoy discovering new products, techniques and processes, but I enjoy it even more when I find something that challenges what I already know.

For example, I remember a dish that I ate in Japan that had a base of tasteless rice. It was shocking because it reminded me of hospital food. The great thing about that dish was that it contained puffer fish gonads and they are one of the most amazing products I know. They were made *yakitori* style with a bit of salt. It was truly spectacular. The contrast between the blandness, hot, very hot and creaminess of that product together with the salt was pure luxury and a very exciting moment for me. I would never have expected that such an extreme blandness was something those chefs would specifically look for, and this realization moved me.

A REFLECTION OF SOCIETY

We as a society now know and recognize the implications that eating has on the life we live, the way in which we behave and the impact these actions have on the planet we inhabit. Therefore, I believe we are moving towards a more responsible gastronomy, which reflects the overall movement of society to more responsible living.

Chan Yan Tak

BORN IN:

Hong Kong SAR, China

BASED IN:

Hong Kong SAR, China

EXPERIENCE:

54 years

SELECT ACCOLADES:

Lung King Heen | 97.00/100 in La Liste (2019)

Lung King Heen | 3 Michelin Stars (2019)

Lung King Heen | No. 80 on the World's 50 Best (2018)

All Photos Courtesy of Lung King Heen

> **"I look for inspiration in my daily life, or when I travel, but I avoid eating at other high-end Chinese restaurants. I don't want to be influenced by other people's creations."**

THE PRAGMATIC CHOICE

My father passed away when I was 13 years old. As the eldest son, it was my responsibility to support the family financially and emotionally. At the time, being a chef was a rational choice as they offered free accommodation and meals for staff. Life wasn't exactly easy, as being a junior chef was all about endurance and patience. Back in those days, becoming a chef was more pragmatic than following a dream.

LIFE OF A CHEF

My first job was with Dai Sam Yuen, a famous restaurant that used to be in the Wan Chai District of Hong Kong. I was a trainee and my role involved cleaning, preparing ingredients, and assisting chefs during banquets in private homes. Sometimes I worked until 2AM, but that was the life of a chef. Ever since I was young, I was prepared for such a life, and I knew the only way to achieve big things was through hard work and dedication.

SHARE THE WISDOM

One of the most important leadership lessons I've learned throughout my career is to help your staff grow and learn. Traditionally, in a Chinese kitchen you only learn by observing other senior chefs cook while you continue doing your assigned tasks. How much you learn depends on how much you can absorb while multi-tasking. At Lung King Heen, after peak lunch hours, our senior chefs stay behind and dedicate time to teaching young chefs various skills and techniques.

A CULTURE OF RESPECT

Historically, you hear more shouting in a Chinese kitchen than words of affirmation. Because I experienced it the hard way, I want my staff to feel respected and happy at work. We always have late night suppers together, and this culture of respect is why we have very low turnover at our restaurant. Some of my colleagues have worked with me for 30 years. If you treat your staff well, they won't be

easily tempted by outside opportunities, as money is not the only priority. They prefer a healthy working environment.

THE PERFECT DISH

Crispy scallops with fresh pear, shrimp paste and Yunnan ham is one of my signature dishes. It is essentially shrimp paste sandwiched between a piece of fresh pear and a piece of scallop, then deep fried. During the creation process, I used banana as the fruit, but then took the advice of my team and replaced it with a pear, giving the dish a crunchy and sweet texture. It swiftly became a classic. When Lung King Heen first opened, this dish was not on the menu, but after lunch I would go around the restaurant and collect feedback from my guests and my regulars requested that we put it back on. If the perfect dish exists, I believe it is one that receives repeated requests to be served. For the past 12 years, this dish is still loved by guests from all over the world.

KEY CHALLENGES

When running a restaurant like Lung King Heen, our biggest challenges are tied to sourcing and consistency. We fly in the freshest products from all over the world and we know what ingredients work best for each specific dish. For example, Kagoshima Chami pork for the pork dumplings and shrimp from Vietnam for the shrimp dumplings. Some of our guests ask why, after trying at home, they can't recreate these dishes with the same recipe. I would say it has to do with the ingredients and their freshness.

AIRPLANE INSPIRATION

Cantonese chefs have become very inventive since the 80s, which is when Hong Kong's economy was on the rise. At the time, I was the Executive Chef of Lai Ching Heen, a Chinese restaurant at the Regent Hotel in Hong Kong. I was required to think of 20 new dishes every month. I just had to find inspiration from what was around me. Sometimes it was by trial and error, and other times ideas were generated by brainstorming with my team. For example, I was on a flight and thought I ordered noodles, but when I peeled open the foil, it turned out to be these long grains that were quite chewy—something I later learned was an Italian pasta called *puntalette* with minced beef in X.O. sauce. I tried cooking this pasta the Chinese way, and this new twist to fried rice has become very popular at Lung King Heen.

STUBBORNLY ORIGINAL

I look for inspiration in my daily life, or when I travel, but I avoid eating at other high-end Chinese restaurants. I don't want to be influenced by other people's creations. I do travel to Singapore and China and eat at local establishments, but I rarely go to competitor or fine dining restaurants because if something tastes good, I don't want to subconsciously copy their idea. I want to remain as original as possible.

MIND TO PLATE

One of my favorite dishes is the baked whole abalone puff with diced chicken. The inspiration behind this dish came from the traditional Chinese bridal cake, of which there is one type named abalone puff—only because the shape of the pastry resembles an abalone. I thought maybe I could make a dim sum that consists of an actual abalone. After some experimentation, the result was an outer pastry puff filled with diced chicken and mushroom, and a 15-head abalone from South Africa nestled atop the fillings. This became one of the restaurant's most requested dim sum.

LOOKING AHEAD

The future of food is intimately tied to good ingredients and seasonality. In the 90s, a trend was started where people looked for dramatic plating and presentation, but that's not my style because if you spend too much time caring about the aesthetic of the plate, the food will become cold. In Cantonese cuisine, the temperature of the food is very important. It can't be lukewarm. It must be steaming hot.

Cristina Bowerman

BORN IN:

Rome, Italy

BASED IN:

Rome, Italy

EXPERIENCE:

15 years

SELECT ACCOLADES:

Glass Hostaria | 1 Michelin Star (2019)

Photo to the Left by Andrea Federici

"I learn all I can from different traditions and combine them with the best Italian cuisine has to offer."

DESTINED FOR ROME

I've been cooking since I was a kid. It is the ultimate freedom. I would cook for friends as a hobby, too. Professionally, however, all my creativity poured out in my role as a graphic designer. I thought to myself that I could apply my creativity in the kitchen as well and decided to change careers at 32—enrolling in Cordon Bleu College in Austin, Texas. I gave myself 10 years to succeed as a chef.

After graduation I wanted to open my own restaurant in Austin, but I needed an edge to convince investors, so I went to Italy to learn how to make fresh pasta in a professional environment. After six months, I was offered a job in Rome. Ultimately, I ended up taking 50 percent in a company that managed a restaurant and a catering business. Then in 2009, three years after opening Glass Hostaria in Rome, we were awarded a Michelin star.

A MAN'S WORLD

I was, and still am, a professional chef in a man's world and I remember vividly how I was treated by my peers at the beginning of my career. Some of them could not see my talent. Others did not realize I was willing to study and work 20 hours a day to become a good cook first and a good chef second. My degree in law, my studies of foreign languages, and my job as a graphic designer helped me speed up the learning curve.

THE TOUGHEST JOB

Being a leader means not only knowing how to lead by example, but also, and above all, being able to motivate every person on your team to give you the best they have to offer. Nowadays, the most difficult job is tied to human resources: trying to inspire people to do their absolute best is a defining feature of true leadership.

A DELICATE BALANCE

I try to balance tradition with new flavors and techniques. Italy has a great heritage of ingredients and recipes, but there is so much more in the world. I love traveling and have had the chance to savor delicious food and incredible products in many different places. I learn all I can from different traditions and combine them with the best Italian cuisine has to offer.

Photo by Giovanna Di LIsciandro

LEARNING AS FUEL

Inspiration comes from what we don't know, and I'm inspired the most when I travel. I perfectly admit that there are a million things I don't know, and that's why as a kid I made a promise to myself to learn something new every single day. It could be a word in a foreign language, or something else entirely, but a hunger to learn is fuel for inspiration and creativity.

MIND TO PLATE

My process of creating a new dish is similar across the board. I focus on one ingredient and then I start to think about what it can be paired with. I try to break the rules and do something nobody has done before, because otherwise it would just be any other dish. I then put three or four ingredients that I like together that could create a flavor profile of that dish, before drawing every element on the plate and how it should be served. If I like the taste, I keep working on it, and if I don't, I start all over again.

A TRIBUTE TO GRANDMA

My favorite dish, even today, is my grandmother's pasta and peas. One of the dishes that will remain in Glass' history is the tagliatelle with cream, ham and peas, where nothing you see is what it seems. This recipe is dedicated to my grandmother's dish that, in any case, will always be better.

CHANGE IS GOOD

I do not believe in eternal dishes. There are great recipes that will remain great, for nothing will ever be better than my grandmother's pasta and peas. That's why I've taken these very recipes and added my own personal touch. I feel the same way about the dishes I've created. They can be modified, refined and built on as time goes on.

A BEAUTIFUL PLATE

Presentation of a dish is very important to me. I worked in graphic design for ten years before pursuing my culinary dream, so the plate needs to be beautiful. The aesthetic part of the experience is not as important as the flavor so the perfect dish, for me, is a balance between the two.

MORE THAN FOOD

Through food you can penetrate minds. In Northern Europe, Spain and elsewhere, food has changed the economy and the way people approach life. It has given us women a way to reach equality. I think Italian cuisine in particular is becoming more structured and is ready to be propelled into the world. It is rich in flavor and history, and is a prime example of how food can become a cultural expression. Chefs like Massimo Bottura are leading the way with innovative cuisine that digs deep down memory lane. The Proustian concept of equating cooking with memory is alive and kicking.

Photos to the Right (top to bottom):
by Giovanna Di LIsciandro
by Andrea Federico
by Niko Boi

David Kinch

BORN IN:

Philadelphia, PA, USA

BASED IN:

Los Gatos, CA, USA

EXPERIENCE:

41 years

SELECT ACCOLADES:

Manresa | 95.25/100 in La Liste (2019)

Manresa | 3 Michelin Stars (2019)

> **"The truth is that satisfaction is attained through the pursuit of perfection, and not through the achievement."**

EXPERIENTIAL LEARNING

When I was young, I moved to New Orleans, Louisiana, and it made a lasting impression—introducing me to how the restaurant scene could be an integral part of a culture. In 1992, I returned to France for my second staging period, and spent the harvest season at a small wine domaine in Chavignol in France's Loire Valley. Following that, I staged with Marc Meneau at a three Michelin-starred restaurant called L'Espérance, in Germany at a now-closed two Michelin-starred restaurant called Schweizer Stuben, and at Akelarre in San Sebastián, which had two Michelin stars at the time. Now it has three. All of these experiences inspired me along my journey.

BREAKING BREAD

I've learned that it's important to rely on my chef de cuisine. While I set the overarching vision, I want everyone to make a contribution, and for the chef de cuisine to put their particular stamp on the food—playing a role in the collaborative process. Another learning comes from our bread program. I was baking the bread for the restaurant and delegated this work to a young cook, Avery Ruzicka, who was schooled in the art of bread-baking. She did such an excellent job that she not only took over the Manresa's bread program, but her work turned out to be the genesis for our signature Manresa Bread and a stand-alone bakery concept with a commissary, as well as three café locations.

THE BIGGER PICTURE

I think the older you get the tougher it is to embrace the kitchen mentality of "work at all costs." Yes, it's important for me to be working hard, but it's also important for me to be resting hard as well. I don't regard kitchen situations as life or death, and I don't sweat the small stuff. Instead, I focus on the bigger picture. I also try very hard to take care of myself by sleeping right and eating right. I'm also of the philosophy that when you are away from the restaurant you should work to find balance.

NEVER AS BAD, NEVER AS GOOD

If we receive criticism from a paying customer, we do whatever we can within reason to correct the problem right away while they are at the restaurant. If we learn afterwards about criticism through communication, we do what we need to get them to come back to the restaurant and give us another

chance. In terms of criticism in public forums, I don't let that bother me. I think everyone is entitled to their own opinion. With respect to critics, some get it and some don't, and I factor that in when reading their reviews. I believe we are never as bad as people say we are, and also never as good as people say we are.

THE MOST IMPORTANT THING

I reject the concept of creativity as the supreme value. It's important, but not of utmost importance. The most important thing is the happiness and satisfaction of our guests. Creativity keeps our job interesting. I think creativity can be both innate and something you can teach, and there's a great teaching aspect in my role as a leader of a team. For example, I'm able to instill the concepts and the

vision of what I want to accomplish and see how my team responds. Creativity is only a piece of that.

INSPIRATION FROM ERROR

I look for inspiration in a myriad of places: reading, traveling, museums, markets and dining in the restaurants of my peers. I also find that cooking at home by myself, for myself, is always inspirational. Some of my "a-ha" moments have come from mistakes. The most satisfying ones are when you make a mistake and it leads to the exploration of a new path, and ultimately a new concept. We are always hitting dead ends and encountering moments that make us stop and approach from a different perspective, whether it's changing how something is cooked or adjusting the seasoning.

MIND TO PLATE

When we create a new beta version of a dish, we don't try and make it perfect. We put the components in place and then taste, adjust, and solicit other opinions. Then we look at the ratio, the seasoning, and where a dish will land on the menu. What comes before and after are big factors in the development of a dish. We are also inspired by seasonal change. After waiting for an ingredient for over half a year, you get products back in season and you can't wait to work with them. Then, months later, you get bored just as they are going out of season.

We always revisit dishes from previous years and sometimes build upon those ideas, especially if they caused us great satisfaction. We will never repeat the exact same dish. It is always this year's version.

PURSUIT OF PERFECTION

I don't think there's such a thing as a perfect dish. The notion of perfection is always a struggle. We try to make everything perfect at the restaurant, with every decision we make, all the while acknowledging that perfection does not exist. The truth is that satisfaction is attained through the pursuit of perfection, and not through the achievement.

THE EVOLUTION OF CUISINE

The biggest change between fine dining now and classicism or neo-classicism from 20 years ago is a change in texture. Back then, luxury or fine cooking was defined by softness and richness—tenderness of meats and voluptuous sauces. Nowadays, texture has moved to the forefront, defined by crispness, chewiness, and other contrasting qualities.

Emma Bengtsson

BORN IN:

Falkenberg, Sweden

BASED IN:

New York, NY, USA

EXPERIENCE:

19 years

SELECT ACCOLADES:

Aquavit | 81.75/100 in La Liste (2019)

Aquavit | 2 Michelin Stars (2019)

Photo to the Left by Eric Vitale
All Other Photos by Signe Birck

"Discipline and creativity are intrinsically linked. It's one thing to have an idea and something else entirely to bring it to life. "

THE FAMILY KITCHEN

My mother and grandmother were the two biggest influences that inspired me to become a chef. My grandmother was so satisfied spending her days in the kitchen preparing a dish. Everything was made from scratch. There were no shortcuts and no cans. Her food was made of simple, pure ingredients prepared with a lot of love and time. Learning to love and respect food in its purest form was one of the greatest lessons she imparted on me. What ultimately led me down a culinary path was once I started culinary school, everything clicked, unlike schoolwork. Cooking came naturally, so from then on I knew it was for me.

AN EARLY LESSON

The first time I worked in a fine dining kitchen was as an extern at Edsbacka Krog, one of the only two Michelin-starred kitchens in Sweden at the time. I was utterly terrified on my first day as I didn't quite know what I was walking into. Looking back, however, I was extremely lucky that it was my first experience, because working there not only reaffirmed that I too wanted to run a kitchen of my own of the same caliber, but more importantly it was there where I learned how I wanted my own kitchen to function. At Edsbacka, everyone treated each other like family.

THE POWER OF PATIENCE

As a leader, a big part of how I work to create an open and collaborative environment at Aquavit is by being patient. There are definitely days when that's

not easy, but losing your temper is more counter-productive than taking the time to nurture someone. Another crucial aspect of exercising patience is being open to any and all questions, no matter how silly. Letting anyone on my team ask anything allows me to find ways to help them learn in a way that works best for them. And when you're not afraid to ask questions, you feel as though your voice is heard and valued, and that cannot be overstated.

On the flip side, as head chef, knowing when to ask your team questions and when to let them solve problems for themselves is equally important. The feeling of accomplishment for being able to achieve something on your own is one of the greatest tools of motivation.

DRIVEN BY CREATIVITY

Being creative is always at the forefront of my life as a chef. It's what drives me and what makes coming to work exciting. Food, like art and music, is a special medium through which anything is possible. You should never be afraid to try something new and evolve. Every aspect of what we do in the restaurant is driven by creativity: creating a completely new dish, reinterpreting a classic, using different techniques, or thinking about how a dish should be plated or presented. I am constantly looking at each part of the process and asking what can be done better or different.

AN UNLIKELY CONNECTION

Discipline, or a lot of stubbornness, and creativity are intrinsically linked. It's one thing to have an idea and something else entirely to bring it to life. It takes a lot of trial, error and insight to know when one concept, combination or technique may or may not work. I do believe that creativity is something you're born with. Not that someone can't manage to be successful without it, but it definitely helps if you have that crazy, undefinable side about you.

THE CORE OF A DISH

When it comes to updating a traditional dish and balancing it with new techniques or flavors, I focus on maintaining its DNA and essence. The updat-

ed dish must tie into your memory of eating the traditional dish. There will always be childhood dishes that your mother or grandmother cooked that should never be touched, but then again they are only ever perfect in your memory. For me, that dish is my grandmother's pot roast. No matter how many times I've tried to make it, hers will always be better. Ultimately, the moment a dish doesn't excite you, it needs to evolve.

GET INSPIRED

Inspiration can be found everywhere—from memories of my childhood to cookbooks to walking around Central Park. I wouldn't say it's cut and dry but when it comes to pastry, after the pieces of a savory dish come together through discussion and research, I'll often have an "a-ha" moment in my sleep. I also relish the chance to visit other restaurants and collaborate with other chefs. I'll never cut and paste what another chef does in his or her own restaurant, but there's no better way to get inspired than actually going out to eat.

Customers, too, are a great source of inspiration. Aquavit has been around for 30 years and yet there are people who come into the restaurant every day who don't know what Scandinavian cuisine is. Being able to be an ambassador for my cuisine is a huge motivator. Creating a memorable experience that brings a smile to their face is what inspires me to give everything I can to every service.

BRINGING AN IDEA TO LIFE

When creating a new dish, sometimes I conceptualize it in my mind and it needs some work, but more often than not it can take a few weeks or even a few months to get it right. Collaboration is the key to getting an idea to the plate, which is a process I like to challenge my team with. Working together will ensure that the ultimate dish will be better than any original instinct I had. Timing, too, is very much tied to how an idea is brought to life.

For example, I was working on this salmon dish for a couple of weeks and it never came out the way I wanted, so I put it on hold. Several weeks went by and I was at the green market and saw some lovage, which is when the dish came together. Having the season change and seeing the lovage got me motivated to try again, but in a whole different direction.

IMPERFECTLY GOOD

The perfect dish only exists in memory, but each dish goes through phases of perfection that are fleeting. For instance, there are dishes that have been on the menu since I started at Aquavit eight years ago that I believe are still great, but one day I might look at those same dishes and think they need to change. The Arctic Bird's Nest, one of the first desserts I had on the menu, looks entirely different today than it did when it was first served. A dish is never perfect, just as people are never perfect. It's about change and evolution. There isn't anything in the world that's perfect, and that's a good thing.

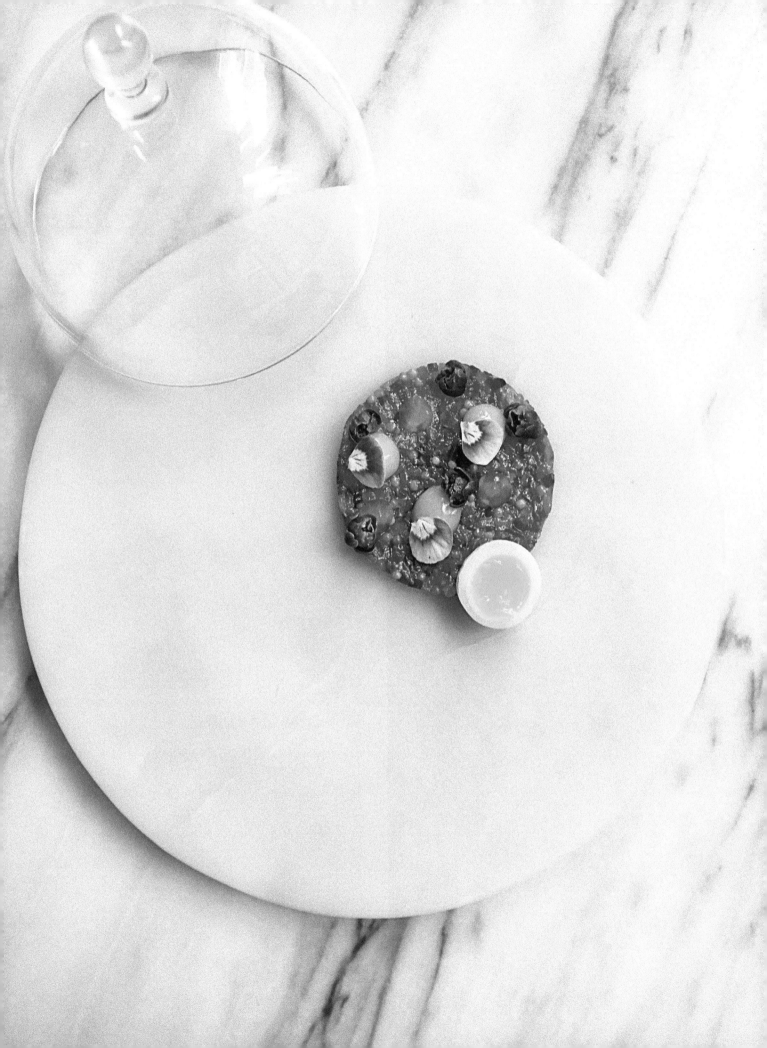

Emmanuel Stroobant

BORN IN:

Liège, Belgium

BASED IN:

Singapore

EXPERIENCE:

34 years

SELECT ACCOLADES:

Shoukouwa | 80.00/100 in La Liste (2019)

Shoukouwa | 2 Michelin Stars (2018)

Saint Pierre | 1 Michelin Star (2018)

Photo to the Left by Edmond Ho

> **"Often times my best ideas come at night, and when something particularly interesting strikes, I will SMS myself so I don't forget."**

CHANGE OF HEART

My studies in criminal law brought me to the doorstep of the culinary world. I needed money and landing a job washing dishes was the only role I could find with no prior work experience. Under the mentorship of Chef Francis Dernouchamp, my interest in the kitchen scene burgeoned into a passion. Instead of becoming a lawyer, I wanted to become a chef. I fell in love with the kitchen ambience, the martial discipline, the team spirit, and the respect that permeated the creation of every dish to be placed on the table of every single restaurant guest.

A VIRTUOUS CYCLE

My first job was in a two Michelin-starred restaurant, and part of my training was being apprenticed out to different restaurants to gain experience. These visits to other venues served to strengthen my choice of career path. I enjoyed the adrenaline rush and excitement of a busy kitchen. It was enthralling to be one component of all the different moving parts, working harmoniously during a busy shift to produce quality dishes. The built-up momentum from the kitchen spilled out to the floor, ensuring guests had an enjoyable experience. I found this cycle invigorating.

Photo by Edmond Ho

ALL FOR ONE, ONE FOR ALL

My own mantra, and one that I impart to my entire team, is based on focus, balance and creativity. These key ingredients are not only important for sustaining a business, but also attributes to embrace in our daily lives. For me, the right attitude will always trump skill. Skills can be taught, but possessing the right attitude can only come from a willingness to learn with patience, passion and integrity. Cooking is a collaborative effort, and in the end, my team understands that we grow, win or fail together.

THE GEM OF AN ORGANIZATION

Nothing transcends the complexities of dealing with a fellow human being, be they a customer, employee, friend or foe. The fact that no one is exactly alike compounds this challenge. My essential benchmarks for successful business dealings and human interaction have always been rooted in trust, commitment and respect. I need to trust my team, my partners and my suppliers, and they in turn need to trust us to be the very best in our endeavors. When there is mutual respect between colleagues, suppliers, customers and even the ingredients you handle, the virtue of dedication will arise. A dedicated team player is an organization's gem.

CREATIVITY NEEDS PURPOSE

Creative cooking must go hand-in-hand with in-depth technical know-how and product proficiency. True creativity stems from having less, rather than from delving into a splurge of ingredients that would result in either a hit or miss. The ultimate aim is to unearth flavors of a main ingredient to

Photo to the Left by Edmond Ho

a level that equates with excellence. I am a strong believer in creative discipline—one must not have carte blanche in meaningless concoctions all in the name of creativity. There are, of course, chefs who are naturally talented with an innate sense of taste, but great chefs have also hailed from those who are willing to work at their craft with passion and dedication.

INSPIRATION IS EVERYWHERE

My culinary philosophy is never to limit my creations to the confines of what I know or can do. My creative juices, more often than not, flow from a happy place, but I'm still trying to figure out how my mind works. I conceptualize better in a calm environment, but the seed for that conception may have taken root from anywhere—an event, movie, soundtrack, fragrance, my daughters' chatter, a family outing to the beach, an art museum, visiting other restaurants, traveling or something else entirely. Inspiration is everywhere and ideas can fly in from any direction.

Photo by Edmond Ho

WALL OF IDEAS

Often times the best ideas come at night, and when something particularly interesting strikes, I will SMS myself so I don't forget. We may not always have the time to develop these ideas immediately, as the ingredients may not be in season or we simply lack the equipment, but after we discuss them as a team, we post our thoughts on our wall of ideas to keep track.

For example, we have a popular hairy crab dish. Instead of trying to source the well-known Shanghainese hairy crab, which was not in season, we looked at the Japanese Hokkaido hairy crab that was readily available. We then used a corn-lemongrass nage that was originally made for another dish. We attempted to pair different sauces with the crab as well as use different cooking methods. After several trials, the end result was something unique and delicious.

PERFECTION IS SUBJECTIVE

There can never be a perfect dish, but there can be perfect moments as judgment of food will always be subjective. Our craft is a process of continuous evolution, be it how a dish has evolved, a person's life journey, or even the evolution in the direction of the company. Saint Pierre's menu today is very different from when the restaurant first started, as my life journey has evolved: from being born in Europe to now calling Asia home. I remember when I first set foot on Asian soil, I was absolutely intrigued with the rich choice of local ingredients.

A MEATLESS FUTURE

For the immediate future, I see my guests trending towards our vegetarian selections. I foresee that there will be a growth of more Michelin-starred vegetarian restaurants, especially with people embracing more and more vegetable-based ingredients. In fact, with school curriculum now covering sustainability and environmental protection, the future generation will perhaps readily welcome a more wholesome lifestyle and we in the culinary world will just have to follow suit.

A GRUELING REALITY

I would advise culinary students and graduates just starting their journey to be very sure they know what being a chef is all about. Many these days are enamored by the glamour that is hyped by the media. They yearn for the quick fix and rise to recognition that really only takes place in their heads. The reality can be so grueling and unkind that many are laid by the wayside. Attitude is the all-encompassing attribute. When you have the right attitude, you'll be blessed to do the right thing intuitively. You will know that patience is the key to success, and that continued curiosity is a natural propellant. Combine these three disciplines together and you just might create something extraordinary.

Photo to the Right by Joyce of Cactus Studio

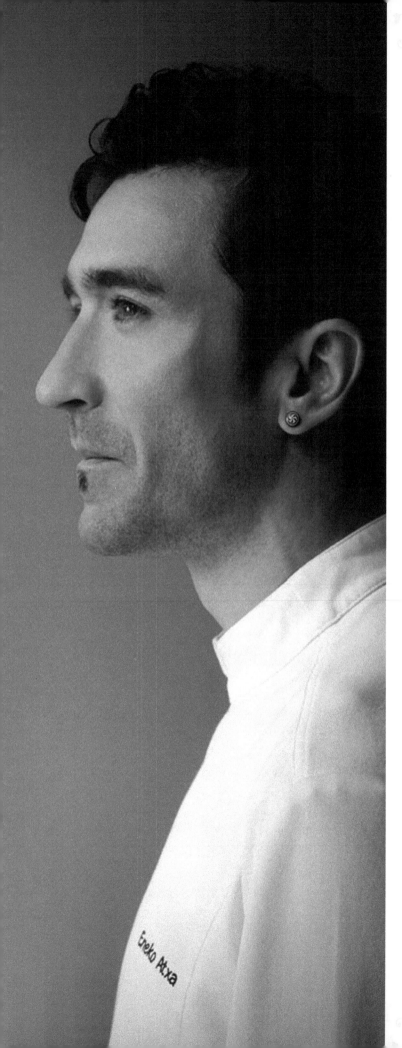

Eneko Atxa Azurmendi

BORN IN:

Bilbao, Spain

BASED IN:

Larrabetzu, Spain

EXPERIENCE:

25 years

SELECT ACCOLADES:

Azurmendi | 98.25/100 in La Liste (2019)

Azurmendi | 3 Michelin Stars (2019)

Azurmendi | No. 43 on the World's 50 Best (2018)

All Photos Courtesy of Azurmendi

> **"Before opening the restaurant every day, we must divest ourselves of every accolade from the day before, the month before, and the year before. We must feel naked of prestige and earn that respect anew."**

THE LANGUAGE OF FOOD

In the beginning my idea of cooking was very simple and routine, but I quickly realized that behind the kitchen there was immense knowledge, technique and insight to learn from, and this type of learning has no end. I realized that cooking, and the world of cuisine more generally, is not simply replicating the recipes of others. Instead, I could compose my own recipes, create my own style, and transmit my own understanding of pleasure, life, identity and culture—all through the language of food.

A SHARED DREAM

One of the most important leadership lessons I've learned is that you and your team must always be on the same page. First, you have to create a dream, and then you share that dream with the people who will help you build it. The dream belongs to everyone. A shared dream requires respect and trust among the team. You must also remember that you were once in the shoes of your colleagues, and it's important to keep that perspective when leading.

NAKED OF PRESTIGE

Before opening the restaurant every day, we must divest ourselves of every award, accolade, recognition and good review from the day before, the month before, and the year before. We must feel naked of prestige when we open the doors to guests who will be with us that day, and we must earn that respect anew. People expect the best from us today, not yesterday. One of the ways we try to ensure consistency is being obsessed with, and very demanding of, small and big details. This minimizes any margin of error.

OUR PHILOSOPHY

I don't believe in being labeled as creative or a master of avant-garde cooking. What is it to be creative? Someone who creates something new everyday? Someone who creates something absolutely artistic or absolutely radical? How do we measure creativity?

At Azurmendi, we are very clear on our philosophy and approach: we don't believe in radical

changes from one day to the next. We believe in reflection, in observation, and in calmness. We believe in constant but incremental change. Our motto is that we cannot change great things every day, but we can change small things, and at the end of the year, 365 small changes add up to something transformative. That's how we stay in motion. The starting point of our continual evolution is always our DNA—culture, identity, territory, birthplace and our way of understanding the world.

INSPIRED BY THE SEASONS

Thanks to this wonderful profession, I am lucky to have had the opportunity to travel the world and visit many professional colleagues, tour many markets, and taste many different traditional, modern and regional cuisines. I learn from all of these experiences, but without a doubt, I am inspired above all by what nature showcases each season. I am privileged to live so close to the sea,

the mountains, and the countryside, and to have four distinct seasons. This gives me a wide variety of products to experiment with all year.

In addition, I come from a place that has a very expansive gastronomic and culinary tradition. These are often the starting points of inspiration. Once I discover which products are available in any given season, I channel my sensory memory to play with textures, aromas and other things that have stirred me from my childhood to adulthood.

NEVER FINISHED

Every single dish we make ends up being different from its initial idea. Dishes are alive. They are never finished. Every day we retouch them and look for ways in which they can evolve. For us, dishes are living elements that are constantly changing, so the dish continues to be developed over time.

MIND TO PLATE

When creating a new dish, I imagine an odor, a texture, or something very beautiful. I imagine the scenography of the plate, and then start to draw it. Once drawn, I show it to my team and explain the intention behind the dream and imagery. Based on this, we bring in various products and begin to build the dream, little by little. The dish starts to have a life of its own. After testing it, we present it to the public and it can be included in any of our menus.

But being on the menu doesn't mean the dish remains static. It continues to change. It never dies. It evolves based on how we think it can be improved, based on customer feedback, and based on how the dish behaves. The perfect dish doesn't exist because every dish continues to develop precisely due to its imperfection.

THE NEXT GENERATION

I would advise those interested in becoming a chef to dedicate themselves to the profession with the utmost passion. They should understand that we are not cooking dishes, but a better future. The next generation of chefs will carry out the next culinary revolution. It will not be tied to techniques, to nouvelle cuisine, to new Basque cuisine, or what Ferran Adrià did. The next generation will have to employ a different kind of revolution: one that takes their passion, learning and drive to help us eat better in hospitals and schools, and to reduce waste in our food chain. In other words, they will have to revolutionize not only the world of gastronomy, but the world at large.

Enrico Crippa

BORN IN:

Carate Brianza, Italy

BASED IN:

Alba, Italy

EXPERIENCE:

30 years

SELECT ACCOLADES:

Piazza Duomo | 95.25/100 in La Liste (2019)

Piazza Duomo | 3 Michelin Stars (2019)

Piazza Duomo | No. 16 on the World's
50 Best (2018)

Photo to the Left by Bruno Murialdo

> **"A dish can be simmering in the background of my mind for a whole year, or it could be created after a few hours of intense concentration."**

A FAMILY AFFAIR

Since I was a child, I spent the summer holidays with my grandfather Attilio, who was my greatest source of inspiration. Every day I would accompany him to the market to select simple and wholesome raw materials. I would sit and watch him for hours cooking in the intimacy of his kitchen, and to this day I remember the aromas and flavors of dishes he prepared.

MY DESTINY

My first experience in the kitchen was under Gualtiero Marchesi, a master of an entire generation of Italian and European chefs. It was a significant experience of my early career. I understood immediately that I had undertaken the right path for my personal and professional growth. This was, is, and will always be my life.

NEITHER PERFECTION, NOR SUCCESS

I always believed that leadership is a form of teaching and being engaged. How can I ask my team to sacrifice if I don't get my own hands dirty? The key lies in not seeking perfection nor success, but rather trying to do better today than we did yesterday, and trying to do better tomorrow than we did today. With this attitude, focus and attention to detail, enthusiasm can be maintained. As a leader, you must not only correct the errors of others, but do so in a way that explains what went wrong and how not to repeat the same mistake twice. This is the only way one can learn and grow.

SAFETY VALVE

Prizes, awards and recognition are constant incentives to do better. And the stress and pressure of accolades are the bread and butter of our work, but I learned to manage this anxiety by finding my safety valve: sports. As soon as I can get on my bike for a few hours, away from my daily commitments, I come back to my center.

22 JUDGES A DAY

Every day we are reviewed several times. In my opinion, each table is a single judge. Therefore, in a restaurant like Piazza Duomo, with just 11 tables serving lunch and dinner, we are theoretically judged 22 times each day. Criticism more generally is always a starting point to improve and find new points of view. We learned to treasure that kind of feedback so that we can constantly get better. For everything to run smoothly, however, there are some fundamental elements that are necessary in every kitchen, team and mind of a chef: absolute respect for raw material, love of research to discover new techniques, influences and ingredients, and the will to do well, get involved and create something special.

CONTROLLING CREATIVITY

Creativity is a fundamental part of my life as a chef, and I think of it as an innate gift. It is something that you cannot explain, teach or pass on. When creating a new dish, there is no real beginning of the creative process. An idea can be born while I'm eating dinner, while I'm cooking, or while I'm riding my bike over the hills surrounding Alba. Once an idea can be articulated and visualized, the creative process moves into a phase of discipline where experimentation and testing take center stage. Because the creative process cannot be controlled, there are periods where I have many ideas and there are periods that are decidedly quieter.

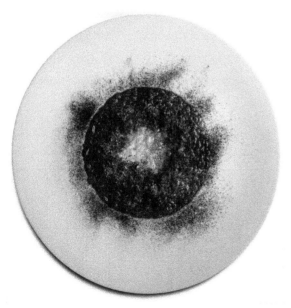

Photo by Lido Vannucchi

MIND TO PLATE

If I sit with my team, in front of a blank piece of paper, we will never get out of the rabbit hole. A dish can be simmering in the background of my mind for a whole year, or it could be created after a few hours of intense concentration. Often, the first idea that occurs to me is not what the end result looks like. An idea can start as a savory dish and finish as a dessert, or vice versa. The limitlessness of creativity allows for such freedom and transformation.

A LOCAL MEMORY

One of our most famous dishes is the potato cream and *lapsang souchong*, which is a black tea originally from the mountainous Wuyi region in the province of Fujian in China. This dish was inspired by the smell of wood burning in the stove, which is typical of rural houses in Piedmont. While some ideas, like this particular dish, have a short production process, other ideas can take far longer to realize. There are many ideas in the pipeline that, but for a small detail, we would bring to fruition. I prefer to wait until we have the complete picture, rather than produce something that does not convince me, even if the shortfall is infinitesimally small.

A HIGHLY COMPLEX PROCESS

If you think about the choreography of a dish, its chromatic aspects, and the balance of tastes orchestrated in such a way to provoke a set of emotions, it is a highly complex process. My culinary philosophy is inspired by the rhythm of the seasons and, given their susceptibility, a dish can take on different aspects with the passing moments of nature. When one element of a dish changes, this re-

Photo by Stefania Spadoni

sults in a total change of creation. For example, we have a dish called Salad 21, 31, 41, 51. The perfection of this dish can be the crunchiness of a small carrot, the softness of a particularly fleshy leaf, or the sweetness of an extraordinarily fragrant flower. Therefore, the definition of perfect is elusive and can mean many things to many different people.

A SEASONAL ENDEAVOR

At Piazza Duomo we have dishes that we never change because our customers love them, and then we have dishes that last a season or two, and then we have dishes that we serve just for a few days because of a particular texture or singular perfume that surfaces for a brief moment in time. We have this flexibility because our cuisine is strictly linked to seasonality.

THE FUTURE OF FOOD

On the horizon I see more and more attention being paid to green ingredients, to the sustainability of agriculture and breeding farms, and to research to help us manage our natural resources. We decided to pursue a vegetable garden more than ten years ago and the phenomenon of foraging, while ever-present today, still had to be born. I do not believe this is a fad. A journey of awareness and respect for the environment that surrounds us has begun, and I think in the next ten years we will be talking even more about green kitchens and a greater respect for nature.

Éric Frechon

BORN IN:

Corbie, France

BASED IN:

Paris, France

EXPERIENCE:

42 years

SELECT ACCOLADES:

Epicure | 97.25/100 in La Liste (2019)

Epicure | 3 Michelin Stars (2019)

Photo to the Left Courtesy of Le Bristol Paris

> **"The focus should always be quality products, in all their glory, that are treated with respect. An overcooked fish is a fish that died for no reason."**

THE UNTHINKABLE

It was through my father, a fruit and vegetable merchant, and my grandfather, Raoul Frechon, a farmer, that I was schooled in quality products from an early age. Canned and frozen foods were unthinkable at home. Chicken came from the farm next door, fresh fish right off the boat, and during Sunday lunches, we often gathered 30 to 40 family members around the same table. Everyone lent a helping hand.

A CIRCUTIOUS JOURNEY

It was the pursuit of a bicycle that first led me to step into a restaurant kitchen. I was 13 at the time, and in order to buy a bike I was coveting, I sought out a casual job and quickly found work in one of Tréport's restaurants. To raise the necessary sum, I spent all my weekends shucking oysters, waiting on tables and helping make pastry. My culinary journey had begun.

CHEF AS CONDUCTOR

One of the most important leadership lessons I've learned is that you must manage a team the way an opera conductor leads a performance. Everyone has their role and must know how to play it. You must understand the strengths and weaknesses of your colleagues, be willing to provide feedback and coaching, empower them to take on more and more responsibilities, and pass on values and tools necessary for them to grow. It may be stressful, but stress in the kitchen is a positive tool that forces us to give our best, push harder and continually improve.

BE PRESENT

One of the ways in which we maintain such a high quality of food and service is by keeping a watchful eye on everything that goes on—from the initial receipt of the products to plating and serving the dish. Creation is a daily challenge and I am always re-evaluating myself as to whether I am giving the best dish I can every day. Being present in the kitchen and always checking the work are essential ingredients to consistency and to successfully leading a team.

SERVING A DREAM

One of the biggest challenges to leading a restaurant such as Epicure is the rigor demanded every

Photo Courtesy of Safran Paris

day for every plate. What helps us overcome this challenge is our passion behind the craft. A chef must never let go of this passion and always strive to provide guests with a dreamlike experience. When guests come to Epicure, they challenge us all to give them an unforgettable memory of their experience throughout the degustation, which is crafted in careful detail: a surprising plate, attentive service, warm environment and balanced decoration. Stepping into our restaurant must be a timeless moment.

BALANCING OLD AND NEW

One of the most important things to renewing ones creativity is to be contemporary while remaining classic. For example, when creating a traditional meal, I integrate new techniques while maintaining the original taste, the elegance of the dish, and its finesse. At the same time, I will introduce a modern visual that surprises guests. My main source of inspiration remains the product itself. I also seek new ideas from what I hear around me, photography, and of course the local market. Ultimately,

when experimenting with old and new, I will never change a plate on the menu for something lesser.

A FLAWLESS TRANSITION

When I design a menu, it's important for me to balance the flavors and the products so that there is a flow and history to the experience. There is never the same texture or taste twice. The menu must not be too heavy so that the diner can appreciate each course until dessert. For example, I always try to balance the menu by offering a vegetable and a crustacean for the entrée, meat or fish for the main course, a selection of cheese—which is very important and represents a nice transition—and then finally a chocolate dessert or seasonal fruit.

UNIQUE COMBINATIONS

I enjoy pairing atypical ingredients that no one would have dared dream of, such as the association of sweetbreads and oysters, which was one of our most successful pairings. In general, pairings between land and sea are atypical and still surprise our guests. When creating a new dish, often we recreate a recipe up to 20 times before we are satisfied with the outcome. This process is a lot of trial and error, and sometimes involves a step back, rather than a step forward.

A MOVING TARGET

Because taste is not universal, each guest can point to his or her own perfect dish, but objectively, perfection cannot be defined. While we consider each dish on Epicure's menu to be perfect, it is always being questioned, revised and improved. Perfec-

tion cannot be static. Cuisine is always evolving and improving, so too must perfection.

STAYING PURE

I find recent developments in gastronomy a bit too fast for my taste. Nowadays you can find most French or international products at any time of the year, but the production of these products to ensure their availability diminishes their quality. The focus should always be quality products, in all their glory, that are treated with respect. An overcooked fish is a fish that died for no reason. My cuisine does not seek to follow trends. Gastronomes flock to Epicure to enjoy a timeless and unforgettable cuisine, and I have never adapted my cooking to the whims of the moment.

Eric Ripert

BORN IN:

Antibes, France

Eric Ripert
Le Bernardin

BASED IN:

New York, NY, USA

EXPERIENCE:

35 years

SELECT ACCOLADES:

Le Bernardin | No. 1 in the World / 99.75/100 in La Liste (2019)

Le Bernardin | 3 Michelin Stars (2019)

Le Bernardin | No. 26 on the World's 50 Best (2018)

Photo to the Left by Nigel Parry
All Other Photos by Daniel Krieger

> **"Mastering the flavors and elements of a new dish can take days, months or even years. I once had an idea for stuffed calamari and it took me twenty years to make it exactly the way I wanted it."**

CULINARY SCHOOL AT LAST

Every day my mother would prepare lunch and dinner as you would experience in a nice restaurant: she would set the table starting with a fresh tablecloth, silverware, china, candles, and flowers. There was always an appetizer, main course, and dessert. She was very inspired by nouvelle cuisine, so I acquired a taste for fine dining early on. I was very lucky. I had this idea that if I worked in a kitchen then I would get to eat all the time. At 15, I was kicked out of school and told that I needed to find a vocation. I tried to look sad, but I was delighted. Culinary school at last.

WHERE'S THE HAMMER?

When I think of my early days in the kitchen, the stories of my challenges always come to mind first. For example, I was training in between my first and second years of culinary school when my chef handed me about 25 ducks, asking me to debone them all, confit the legs, then freeze the breasts. A week later, the chef asked me for one of the frozen breasts. I returned to him holding a boulder of almost 50 breasts—all frozen into a solid block. We needed a screwdriver and hammer to separate them. The chef did not find it very funny. It's a reminder that everyone starts at the beginning and we all make mistakes as we learn. Never again did I make that mistake.

A LESSON IN RESPECT

I used to be a very authoritative chef. I would yell at my cooks and had very little tolerance and patience. It was the style of management that I experienced during my early years of training. Around 2000, I started to contemplate the kitchen's atmosphere. We were losing a lot of employees and I was confused. I decided to re-evaluate the way in which I managed people and realized something in myself. I couldn't be happy if I was angry. Those emotions cannot coexist. A cook can't make delicious and beautiful food if his hands are shaking from fear. Today, we don't yell in the kitchen, and there is no drama. Even during our busiest times, we have a peaceful environment.

LEARNING IS FOREVER

I try to instill in my team that they remain humble and always continue learning. My mentor and co-founder of Le Bernardin, Gilbert Le Coze, once told me, "If you have a good article, read it once, and never look at it again. If you have a bad article, keep it on your desk and read it every day for a long time, until you correct the mistakes." I feel his advice so succinctly captures the need to always evolve and improve yourself, and to never become stagnant.

THE CHALLENGE OF CONSISTENCY

The greatest challenge to success in a restaurant of our caliber is consistency. Every evening we must ensure that every guest at every table has the best experience possible. Guests often join us for very different reasons—business lunches, celebratory occasions, once-in-a-lifetime splurges—so our team must identify the level of guidance, interaction, and pacing of the meal that our guests desire, while still providing exceptional quality in both service and food. The key to achieving this is communication: between the front of the house and the kitchen, between the maître d', the captains, the waiters, the sommeliers, and anyone else who may "touch" that table.

PASSION BEATS PRESSURE

Handling the pressure of Le Bernardin's many accolades is simple: I forget about the stars and focus on the work. Every morning I wake up and on my way to Le Bernardin I think about what I need to do as a chef. I'm not thinking about maintaining the awards. I believe that if we work hard and focus on the passion that has brought us to where we are, we can hopefully continue our success.

Of course, we celebrate the awards when they happen and are truly honored with all that our dedicated team has achieved, but it's not our daily motivation. Even if we didn't have the recognition that we did, I'd still be happy because I love what the Le Bernardin family and I are doing. If you do something you love, you will never feel any pressure.

THE FISH IS THE STAR

At Le Bernardin, we try not to have signature dishes, and we try to change the menu as much as we can. If you look at our menu each year, you'll realize that 90 percent of it has changed. I always like to evolve with the seasons, as well as take inspiration from the discoveries we make along the way, whether by traveling, studying new techniques, or a sous chef's suggestion. One of our philosophies, passed down from Chef Gilbert Le Coze, still stands: do whatever you want, just do it in Le Bernardin's style. Today, that means remaining true to our defining mantra—the fish is the star of the plate. We encourage our team to play with tradition, techniques, and international flavors as long as every element on the plate is there to elevate and enhance the qualities and characteristics of the seafood.

THE CREATIVE PROCESS

We spend a lot of time creating and experimenting to perfect a new dish. It all begins with a spark of inspiration. I ask my sous chefs, and also impose on myself, to take notes whenever any of us has an idea. I write it down on whatever piece of paper I have nearby. Eventually I bring all of the papers together and carve out a spot conducive to creativity—one that is calm, quiet, and clutter-free. Sometimes we get lucky and it only takes us a few days to master the flavors and elements of a new dish, and other times it takes months. Sometimes, an idea sounds really good and we're excited to pursue it, but when we try it, we realize it's not at all what we expected.

We don't rush ourselves, either. I once had an idea for stuffed calamari and it took me twenty years to make it exactly the way I wanted it. The challenge was to have calamari that was tender and not overcooked, while also having the stuffing cooked inside. It took us forever to find a solution.

SCIENCE + ART

Once the team is content with a dish and it goes on the menu, the next goal is to consistently produce that dish. But that is harder than you might think. Different fish have different properties depending on the time of year, such as the temperature of the water. Cooks must be able to adapt their techniques to the particular qualities of that fish. You can't do the same thing every time. Cooking is a science and an art, and part of the art comes from knowing how to adapt your techniques to your ingredients. If you can't replicate a dish night after night, then it doesn't matter how delicious it was during the initial tasting.

Georgianna Hiliadaki
&
Nikos Roussos

BORN IN:

Athens, Greece

BASED IN:

Athens, Greece

EXPERIENCE:

16 years

SELECT ACCOLADES:

Funky Gourmet | 81.25/100 in La Liste (2019)

Funky Gourmet | 2 Michelin Stars (2018)

All Photos by Katerina Avgerinou

"We see food as a form of art, a culinary experience like going to the theatre or the opera. But above all, taste cannot be sacrificed for creativity."

HOW IT STARTED

Georgianna: I first started cooking when I was six years old, and I still remember asking my mom for some money to buy my first cookbook for children—with recipes from all over the world. Ever since, I've loved helping her in the kitchen. While at university in the United Kingdom, I would always organize grand feasts for my friends, and it was only after graduation that I decided to pursue this passion professionally and studied culinary arts in New York.

Nikos: I would always invite my friends and family over, organizing food parties and paying special attention to plating and styling the food. I then decided to pursue my culinary passion and enrolled in the Institute for Culinary Education in New York.

THE PERFECT ENVIRONMENT

When we first entered a professional kitchen we fell in love with the whole operation. Cooking is one of those fields where a home cook and professional cook are worlds apart. We were both intrigued and excited by the craziness, complexity, fast pace, creativity, accuracy and how demanding it could be.

LEAD BY EXAMPLE

This profession necessitates that you be extremely precise, organized and well-disciplined, in order to demand these traits in others. And when you do manage to create a strong team with similar qualities, you must always be evolving to inspire them, keep them interested, and eventually cultivate a long-lasting professional bond. Fairness and respect are hallmarks of a strong team.

MISTAKES AS FRIENDS

It's the nature of our job to always be under constant criticism, but you always have to filter that criticism before you internalize it. You need to be able to analyze where it's coming from, whether it's genuine or not, and you must also ask yourself what, if anything, went wrong. In the end, our mistakes are our best friends, since they make us better in what we do.

A DUAL JOB

Being a chef-owner can be extremely stressful at times. You must wear two hats. On one hand, you need to keep your creativity strong and alive, and

on the other hand, you need to think about minimizing expenses, the cost of food and staff, and other tasks that are not very creative at all.

THE GREEK SALAD SORBET

Creativity is at the core of everything we do as chefs. At Funky Gourmet, we see food as a form of art, a culinary experience like going to the theater or the opera.

The Greek salad sorbet is the perfect example of our creative process. We had a distilled water of Greek salad on our menu for a few months when we asked ourselves: why don't we freeze this distilled water to see what will happen? The outcome of this exercise was a white sorbet that tasted exactly like a Greek salad. You would see white, but you would taste tomatoes, which sparked a special game of the mind with texture. Other times we go through a lot of trial and error to reach the desired result. The most important thing to keep in mind is that we are handling food, and above all, it must be delicious. Taste cannot be sacrificed for creativity.

MIND TO PLATE

While some ideas are relatively easy to bring to life, others take months to mature before they make it to the menu. A classic example of this is our signature dish, the silence of the lamb. It is one of the most challenging and most delicious plates on our menu: lamb brain cooked sous-vide and finished on the pan with a lemon-oregano sauce in a lamb brain soup. The idea of using lamb brain had been on our mind for ages. We first saw the use of such an underestimated raw material in high-end cuisine at elBulli in 2005. It had a very interesting

texture and taste, and we were very keen on using it but could never figure out how. Then, after three years of experimenting, the plate was perfected and integrated into our degustation menus. It is now one of our delicious signature dishes that repeat guests ask for again and again.

We often try many different things along the way because sometimes a dish can work in terms of taste, but not in terms of appearance—or vice versa. Once a new dish hits the menu, we taste it with our sommelier and discuss what would be the best wine or beverage to accompany it. The wine pairing plays a very important role in the whole culinary experience.

WORDS OF WISDOM

The most important thing you need to know about being a professional chef is that you need to be organized, meticulous, clean, and constantly stirring waters. Chef Ferran Adrià once said you have to be organized in order to be creative, and this simple piece of advice has proved its wisdom many times over throughout our culinary lives.

Guillaume Galliot

Guillaume Galliot

BORN IN:

Chambray-les-Tours, France

BASED IN:

Hong Kong SAR, China

EXPERIENCE:

21 years

SELECT ACCOLADES:

Caprice | 88.25/100 in La Liste (2019)

Caprice | 3 Michelin Stars (2019)

All Photos Courtesy of Caprice

> ## "Over many years, my mind has become a database of ingredients, and that helps my creative synapses connect to find the best combinations of flavors."

CULINARY DESTINY

When I was growing up I would follow Charles Barrier, Alain Ducasse, Joël Robuchon, and Paul Bocuse on TV. I would find every article I could about them to learn more about their ideas, passion and work. I was very inspired by these influential chefs and wanted to cook like they did. In that sense, I always wanted to become a chef, but I was very open to what direction that took. I worked in a brassiere, I did pastry, and I even worked as a cook in a hospital, all in an effort to find the part of this industry that excited me the most.

IGNITED BY THREE STARS

It was not until I went to work for the Pourcel brothers, who had a three Michelin star restaurant at the time, did I truly decide on the kind of chef I wanted to be. They worked in the restaurant every day, and their staff all came from two and three star Michelin restaurants. Working with a team that focused and dedicated helped ignite the passion in me to achieve that same level of excellence in my career.

COACH AND COLLABORATOR

If I taste something one of my cooks made and it is not up to my standard, I don't simply ask them to remake it. I will often cook with them, helping them learn along the way. That is how we challenge ourselves to get better and keep learning. As a manager, I am firm and relaxed at the same time. I have standards that I expect the team to follow and I push them to be better each day. But I would say that how I deliver that message is in the spirit of a coach and collaborator. My team shouldn't come in each day fearful of discipline, but excited to keep growing to the next level, knowing that I will be there to help them along the way.

THE BIGGEST CHALLENGE

Because we are in Hong Kong, and not in France, the logistics of getting the products we need are more complicated. Living on an island we need to import everything, so I need to constantly think about freshness and how to keep the quality of our dishes consistent. The most important features of being successful, however, go beyond the quality of the products. It is about the quality of the team, and the ability to continually create and be creative.

after about one week, I get to a place where I am happy with a new dish. On the other hand, *laksa de crabe et oeuf confit*, a reinterpretation of the classic Singaporean dish, took one month to get right.

Today we have a pigeon dish on the menu that is the result of experimentation and tweaking for years, but only recently did we reach a point where I was convinced that we've taken this dish to a perfect place. The main thing we were trying to perfect was the sauce—looking for just the right balance of acidity and chocolate to balance the gaminess of the pigeon and foie gras that is served alongside the dish. In that sense, I do believe in the perfect dish, and right now, this one fits the bill.

FAD OR PHILOSOPHY

Some trends come and go, and other trends are not trends at all. For instance, people are now quite interested in organic produce and products, but all the food we cooked with and ate growing up in France was organic. So there is a difference between fads

TOMATO AND TRUFFLE

The first step to culinary creativity is having a deep understanding of the products and their seasonality. Once that's in your memory, your brain can start to understand what pairings will work. For example, I would never put tomato and truffle together because I know the seasons don't match. Black truffle with root vegetables, pumpkin, and chestnut—these flavors make sense because they are from the same season. Over many years, my mind has become a database of ingredients, and that helps my creative synapses connect to find the best combinations of flavors.

THE PERFECT DISH

Most of the time when I fall in love with a product, I will order it and start to experiment. Sometimes,

that are driven by marketing, and having a cooking philosophy that you are true to and abide by.

RICH IN KNOWLEDGE

I would advise those pursuing a culinary career to learn all of the basics properly. Do not take shortcuts. You aren't going to know how to run a business by watching a TV show and winning a competition. You might have culinary talent but you don't necessarily understand the business side of the industry. Also, you must look for mentors along the way, as they will be your best teachers and advocates. And once you have done all of this,

know when it is time to break away and work on your own. That's where you will discover your own identity in the kitchen.

Above all else, the most important thing you need to know about being a professional chef is that when you start, you are going to work long hours for no money, but with this experience, you will become rich in knowledge.

Guy Savoy

BORN IN:

Nevers, France

BASED IN:

Paris, France

EXPERIENCE:

49 years

SELECT ACCOLADES:

Guy Savoy | No. 1 in the World /
99.75/100 in La Liste (2019)

Guy Savoy | 3 Michelin Stars (2019)

Photo to the Left Courtesy of Guy Savoy
All Other Photos by Laurence Mouton

> **"The basic ingredients for creativity are passion, desire and a love of food, but equally important are the memories of flavors."**

HOMEMADE BISCUITS

There is a very precise moment I keep in memory of exactly when I fell in love with cooking. It was when I discovered that cookery is the art of lifting food from being merely edible to the realm of pleasure in a matter of moments. This revelation came to me when I was five or six years old. My mother, who always took great care to keep the big tin of homemade biscuits well-stocked, let me make some *langues de chat* biscuits—a light, crunchy French treat. Imitating her, I shaped the little rolls of mixture, laid them on the baking tray, and then watched as they suddenly spread themselves, turning golden around the edges. A few minutes later, after being removed from the oven, the biscuits were crisp, crunchy, and tasting of butter. That memory has lived with me ever since. I realized then that cooking was about transformation.

MESMERIZED BY MOVEMENT

One of the most important moments early on in my career was an apprenticeship with the Troisgros brothers. Their restaurant, La Maison Troisgros in Roanne, France, has been a three Michelin star restaurant for more than 30 consecutive years. This was a pivotal experience for when I watched the chefs pick up a pan, put down a plate, or stir a sauce, their movements were so precise and so beautiful that I longed to reach the point where I could work as they did.

A LESSON FROM RUGBY

Leadership is intimately tied to team spirit, and I learned this from rugby. I came to understand that the winning team was the team that best combined contrasting talents of its players—all working together as one. Today, I view my role as being similar to that of both a rugby captain and coach: my forwards' domain is the kitchen, the dining room is that of my wingers and centers, and my role is to choreograph the play. I direct the service, manage the tempo, delegate the work and maintain a consistent rhythm. No detail is left to chance, and each movement is practiced, honed, and as important as a pass in a Six Nations match.

NO SUBSTITUTE FOR HARD WORK

Hard work is a recipe that never disappoints. There is no substitute. I learned this from my mentors,

who gave their time, effort and enthusiasm to helping me, coaching me, and teaching me to be better and better over the years. Since I was 15 years old, I have worked 16-hour days, and that translates to many decades of toil under my belt. This is due to my passion for the craft, for you must have the utmost dedication to your work to devote such a time commitment. I'm happy to say that this passion has not wavered over the years. And like I always say, passion prevents stress.

A RICH MEMORY BANK

The basic ingredients for creativity are passion, desire and a love of food, but equally important are the memories of flavors. If, for example, you have never tasted a banana, you would be entirely unable to identify its flavor. When creating new dishes, I draw on my *papillothèque*—my own internal library of tastes—where I can experience those flavors once again. It is said that great composers hear music first in their head before they commit to a paper score, or that great perfumers are able to recreate a scent that they have only yet imagined. I believe you could say the same of a chef. I sense a taste and set about finding the right produce, seasonings and cooking techniques that will bring that taste into being.

ICED OYSTERS

The cook's creativity is born of the five senses. Just the sight of an ingredient can give me an idea for a dish, so can a lecture, a song lyric, a story, or a piece of music. They all can give rise to this creative urge. On occasion, the wish to overcome certain obstacles or challenges can lead to creation, as in the case of my first signature dish, *huîtres en nage glacée*, or iced oysters. Whenever I ate oysters, I always felt somewhat disappointed at not being able to taste all the sea water that is found within the shell. So much of it was lost as it ran down your fingers. I began to think about how you might be able to drink this delicious sea water, but I found that the only solution was to eat it, so I solidified the water from the oysters in a jelly, ate the water, and was delighted by the result—as were my guests, I hope!

HEALTHY FEEDBACK

I believe that every entrepreneur labors and creates according to his or her own distinct personality, and as such cannot please everyone. To receive some criticism seems to me a rather healthy notion. Indeed, I have adapted certain behaviors as a result of substantive feedback. Today, after 50 years in the industry, if a reviewer labels me unique, I consider that a mark of success. With regard to failure, I have long stood by the phrase, you learn from your mistakes.

A FUNDAMENTAL TRUTH

The rules that underpin the culinary arts are the foundations without which creativity cannot flourish, and these rules will live on: the calling upon all five senses is, to my mind, a necessity for the future of cuisine, as is the magic of transformation, which itself is the very essence of cooking. Finally, the quality of the produce used and, by extension, the standards of producers and their methods of production will always remain at the forefront of the industry and the profession.

SECRETS OF THE KITCHEN

I would advise young cooks and those interested in pursuing a culinary career to partake in all aspects of gastronomy—feeling, touching, seeing—and in the entire palette of flavors and cooking techniques available to us. They must unlock the secrets of the kitchen.

The best way to hone your skillset is through apprenticeships. The acquisition of these precise crafts demands daily practice. I always tell young chefs that to be a cook is to possess a true skill that is hard-won, and once acquired, has the potential to open up the world. The craft of a cook is held in high esteem. You can choose any location on earth and find gratifying, exciting employment opportunities. You can work alongside men and women who enrich your life with their presence, be they fellow cooks, restaurant guests, suppliers or artists. Cooking is a craft that affords the expression of individual sensitivity and personality, and a craft that elicits boundless enthusiasm.

Hans Neuner

BORN IN:

Leutasch, Austria

BASED IN:

Algarve, Portugal

EXPERIENCE:

28 years

SELECT ACCOLADES:

Ocean | 96.00/100 in La Liste (2019)

Ocean | 2 Michelin Stars (2019)

All Photos Courtesy of Ocean

> ❝From a technical point of view, you can always perfect a dish in terms of cooking point, texture and other features, but true perfection is personal and emotional.❞

A FAMILY AFFAIR

My family has managed restaurants for more than 60 years. It was therefore always clear to me that I would become a chef. Having grown up in a restaurant environment all my life, I developed a passion for cooking at a very young age.

THE EARLY YEARS

When I first started seriously in a professional kitchen, the amount of work was daunting. I spent 12 to 14 hours every day in the kitchen. However, with a solid team, the right products and a true passion for the craft, it has always been a pleasure to work and do this job. I like to say that you should never give up and that you must always believe in yourself.

CORE PILLARS

Earning respect in this world, among your team, colleagues and beyond, comes from several pillars: doing what you know well, leading by example, sharing your knowledge and expertise with others, and by empowering and supporting your team members.

THE HARDEST PART

The key challenges to leading and running a restaurant like Ocean, and to maintaining consistency, include sourcing the absolute perfect products and working together with suppliers who understand your quest for quality; keeping the team focused and always on the right track; and constantly staying creative by getting inspired by our surroundings, travels and colleagues. It's also important for the staff to feel like they are part of the family. We all go for drinks together, we eat together, and I spend time with each of them. Having a shared vision and shared goals is how we continually evolve and advance as a team and as a restaurant.

BEING CREATIVE

Creativity can be innate, for those who are lucky, but I believe it can also be learned over the years through experience and very hard work. Being constantly creative is not easy. Ideas can come to you at any time, but it is also a collaborative process with various team members who bring their own experiences to the table. We can learn an awful lot

from each other and transform one idea into another through constant experimentation. I always encourage feedback and input from the team when we create new dishes, and would rather my team speak up than be quiet.

GETTING INSPIRED

Being curious and traveling enables you to open your mind to other concepts, techniques and products. The age of the Internet has provided a platform for inspiration through photos and videos, and being able to have the visual information of a dish and how it's plated is sharing knowledge. However, instead of copying other things you see, as many chefs do, you must be authentic and stay true to your own identity.

MIND TO PLATE

One of the best examples of creating a new dish is the *queijo de porco* item on the Ocean restaurant menu. On a trip to the north of Portugal, I saw for the first time a piece of pressed pork head meat in a butcher shop. It was called *queijo de porco*, which means pork cheese, even though it doesn't have any cheese in it at all. We decided to play on this and make a dish with pressed pork head meat and make it look like a small cheese. We shaped it, made the mold and covered it with St. Jorge Cheese from the Azores, which is aged 24 months, and makes it look even more like a cheese. It took between four and six weeks until we finished tweaking and were ready to serve it on the menu. To make it look like real cheese, we presented it in a cheese box, which we had specially crafted. It is one of the best dishes on the menu.

STRIVING FOR PERFECTION

I don't believe that a singular perfect dish exists. The perception is different for every person. For me, my brother's goulash is perfect, as it brings back flavors tied to childhood memories, so it's a very personal and individual emotion. Of course, from a technical point of view, you can always perfect a dish in terms of cooking point, texture and other features. As a chef, you are always striving for perfection in everything you do.

THE FUTURE OF FOOD

I believe that humanity has to seriously start thinking differently about food—how it is sourced, pro-cessed, and distributed. We need to use the earth's natural resources intelligently and with sustainability at the forefront of our mind. At Ocean restaurant, we are concerned and more conscious about sustainable fishing and taking care of the oceans. We are starting to do something about it by supporting local fishermen who use traditional techniques, such as line fishing and using traditional local artisans and producers. This keeps the crafts-manship and ancient techniques alive.

More generally, culinary trends come and go. Street food has been a recent trend, but it has always existed and is nothing particularly new. Street food has existed in every culture since time immemorial.

Jacob Jan Boerma

BORN IN:

Höchst, Austria

BASED IN:

Vaassen, The Netherlands

EXPERIENCE:

21 years

SELECT ACCOLADES:

De Leest | 93.25/100 in La Liste (2019)

De Leest | 3 Michelin Stars (2019)

All Photos by Kim Veldman

"Nature rules over our menu, and the seasons decide the quality of the product."

EARLY INSPIRATION

I embarked on a culinary path because of my grandmother. Every Sunday she would prepare a warm lunch of local duck with pumpkin, juniper berries and other ingredients, and it would send a delicious aroma all through the house. This was my first experience of being inspired by food—the scent.

WHERE IT STARTED

I remember working in my first kitchen like it was yesterday. It was a one Michelin star restaurant. I was very nervous, but this is where my love for the work really started. There was incredible discipline among the team and an enormous focus on quality. I realized then that this was the only way to achieve success. Today, discipline is the operative word when understanding success, and staying successful.

A POSITIVE VIRUS

You can only create when you are involved as a chef—day in and day out. In order to maintain enthusiasm among the team, you yourself must remain positive and excited. Only then can you transfer this positive virus to others. In terms of leadership, you are only as effective as your explanation for why you do things a certain way. You must communicate clearly, and often, and have a shared vision for your team and the work. You must also instill in your team that you must never lie about the quality of the product. These ideas and values form the foundation of a healthy team.

ALWAYS ON MY MIND

One of the things that keeps me awake at night is the thought that quantity becomes more important than quality. As a chef you must never give in to that mind-set. Getting the best product there is day after day can only be

is the starting point, but I enjoy enriching Dutch cuisine with flavors and elements from all over the world. While nature guides me, and seasons influence the availability of certain ingredients, nothing can be fresher than regional products. For example, my menu always contains langoustine, but the dish changes every season. The day I feel pressure to cook, rather than being fuelled by natural curiosity, passion and excitement, I will quit being a chef.

MIND TO PLATE

Creating a new dish always begins in my mind. Once I have an idea, we prepare the different elements and through a lot of trial and error we will get to a dish that we ultimately make available to our guests. The turbot, cauliflower and *beurre noisette* is a classic example of this process. Every year I add different elements and tastes, always mindful of the balance of flavors. Sometimes we simply can't get a dish quite right. When I feel that moment is upon us, I quit developing the dish.

NOT FAR OFF

I don't believe that something like the perfect dish exists because everyone has different palates and preferences. However, if guests compliment a standout dish on my menu, perfection can't be far off, and at least I know that the dish is unique in its own right.

LOOKING AHEAD

One of the ways in which our industry is evolving is the need for more accessible restaurants that offer high quality food and a dining experience for an affordable price. Due to the increased popularity

achieved by getting suppliers to care about your standards, and when they do, they become part of your success. Ultimately, a passionate team is the cornerstone of success. Nature rules over our menu, and the seasons decide the quality of the product. But most importantly, flavor is the key. It is the building block for continuity.

THE ESSENCE

When we think about creativity and cooking, creativity decides uniqueness: finding the perfect balance between flavors and textures is a key component in my way of cooking. Whatever you combine, in whatever way, the original flavor of the product should never be lost. Discipline is the basis for my efforts, but creativity allows for my personal touch and for a dish to be in the style of my kitchen.

SOURCE OF INSPIRATION

Art, local markets and traveling to different countries are all sources of inspiration. My own region

of the chef's profession, a lot of emphasis has been taken off the serving staff, so I believe chefs will be interacting with patrons more and more in the future—not just to enhance the dining experience, but also out of necessity. As for the preparation of food, flavors will be emphasized and classical techniques will gain traction. We're moving towards a more honest way of cooking.

ALWAYS A NEED

The most important thing you need to know about being a professional chef is that it is a boundless profession and forever in need. People will always need to eat. So regardless of any technological development, social trend or otherwise, there will always be a demand for food cooked by professionals.

Joachim Wissler

BORN IN:

Nürtingen, Germany

BASED IN:

Bergisch Gladbach, Germany

EXPERIENCE:

35 years

SELECT ACCOLADES:

Vendôme | 98.00/100 in La Liste (2019)

Vendôme | 3 Michelin Stars (2018)

Vendôme | No. 66 on the World's 50 Best (2018)

All Photos Courtesy of Restaurant Vendôme

> **"I can be inspired from the scent of a very special mushroom in a meadow at the edge of the forest in spring. From there, I attempt to express that fragrance in a dish."**

A CALLING

Working at my parents' Spartan Inn, I became acquainted with cooking as a profession for the first time. I was 12 years old, and my life changed from that point on. I helped out with kitchen service at the Inn on weekends, and that was my contribution to the family. I realized very quickly that cooking would not only be a profession, but a calling for the future.

MY OWN WAY

I learned that the job of a chef, as I imagined it then, had nothing to do with my educational experience or the years that followed because I quickly started working at the highest levels of cooking. Looking back, I am very grateful that I made my way as a cook back then without being dominantly imprinted by a famous mentor or another well-known personality. This allowed me to develop my own distinct footprint in the profession, and my very own style of leadership and management.

NATURAL CURIOSITY

The most important lesson I've learned over the years is to realize that your own opinion is a subjective assessment of your own work, which is not always correct. You must constantly learn, experiment, embrace feedback, and adjust accordingly. An eagerness to continually learn is due to my natural curiosity, which is essential to success in this industry.

BEING CONSISTENT

The biggest challenge to success is consistency. Every day the team must meet our tough standards and perform the best possible service. From my experience, past performance of staff is a key indicator of future performance of staff, so a successful service begets another successful service. At the same time, I ensure consistency by being personally involved every day.

MAINTAINING BALANCE

I can be creative in my profession as a chef, like very few people can. It's an elementary part of my being a chef—to try new things every day without forgetting the traditions and experiences of the past. While new techniques are used to enhance flavors, rather than to create visual effects, it is not hard to keep the essence of a dish, while bringing something new and elevated to the table.

SPONTANEOUSLY INSPIRED

I am inspired by nature, the seasons, aromas, memories from childhood and much more. For the most part, I am inspired spontaneously. It is only in a brief moment that you can get a kind of suggestion to try and experience something new. Inspiration cannot be planned—it either happens or it doesn't.

MIND TO PLATE

I can be inspired from the scent of a very special mushroom in a meadow at the edge of the forest in spring on my parents' farm. From there, we attempt to express that fragrance in a dish. All possibilities are worked through until the result is absolutely convincing, or discarded because it simply does not convince. There are many ideas for dishes that did not succeed because the result did not meet my expectations. We have a creative pool of three people who decide what goes on the menu and what doesn't, and once a dish does make it onto the menu, we have a feedback session with the front of house since they are the one's talking to guests.

PERFECT, FOR A MOMENT

The perfect dish is always perfect until someone else makes it even better. One of my signature dishes, for example, that I believe is perfect already is the marinated goose liver with Guanaya dark chocolate, beetroot and popcorn cream. Because we put an inordinate amount of effort into making new dishes and combining ingredients, it's very rare for us to evolve dishes.

TRUE FOOD CULTURE

I live in a country with over 80 million people, of whom probably 0.2 percent or fewer know me. However, I am part of the most important, most beautiful and most elementary cultural heritage of our humanity: food culture. I belong to the people who do not prepare food as a means to an end, namely, to become full, but rather for enjoyment.

If I wanted to present myself via a medium of our age through a particular platform, TV show or social media channel, I am not certain I would reach people who share my ideas of food culture. I don't want to deny that chefs have evolved to have a certain pop star image over the last 20 years, but most of it is mere entertainment, governed by ratings and not by the zeitgeist of our true food culture.

Joan Roca

BORN IN:

Girona, Spain

BASED IN:

Girona, Spain

EXPERIENCE:

35 years

SELECT ACCOLADES:

El Celler de Can Roca | 98.50/100 in
La Liste (2019)

El Celler de Can Roca | 3 Michelin Stars
(2019)

El Celler de Can Roca | No. 2 on the World's
50 Best (2018)

All Photos Courtesy of El Celler de Can Roca

> **"We cook to awaken the senses and emotions. All of our work, research and creativity point to enhancing the guest experience in that direction."**

CHILDHOOD AROMAS

I was raised in a restaurant bar, Can Roca, opened by my parents in 1967 in Taialà—an outlying district of Girona. For me and my brothers, the family restaurant was our living room, the place where the three of us grew up, played heads or tails, and did homework amongst the scents of my mother's kitchen. The scents of my childhood included *escudella i carn d'olla*—a traditional Catalan soup and stew—stocks and, in the afternoon, vanilla custard.

A YOUNG HELPER

After school I loved helping my mother in the kitchen any way I could, and every Tuesday afternoon I made sausages with my father. We minced the meat, and then we seasoned and stuffed it. I practiced so much with the hand mincer that I won every arm-wrestling match in school. Grandma Angeleta, Grandma Francisca and other elderly ladies, friends of the grandmothers, were always in the kitchen peeling garlic, onions or beans, spending the afternoon chatting and solving the problems of the world.

WITHOUT HESITATION

The family restaurant kitchen was, after all, our home kitchen. I enjoyed being in my mother's kitchen so much that as young as nine years old she had a chef jacket tailor made for me. Unknowingly, I was beginning to engineer my future. When the time came I didn't hesitate to decide what I wanted to be when I grew up. I saw that people were happy at my parents' restaurant and I wanted to keep making people happy, following the values my mother instilled in us: generosity, hospitality and hard work.

HUMAN CAPITAL

Cooking is a team sport. You simply cannot achieve greatness alone. Human capital is the most important capital in the restaurant, and we invest heavily in our team and resources to take care of our staff. This enables them to grow and perform their best. In terms of success and recognition, it is more important to be genuine than to be the best in the world.

A WAY OF LIVING

I accepted that the time devoted to cuisine could disconnect me from my family and friends, so the solution was making my profession a way of living—avoiding this separation. That's why I live on top of my restaurant kitchen, or I have my restaurant kitchen under my house.

MANAGING A COMPLEX TEAM

One of the challenges I've had to manage over the years stems from working in a small kitchen with two people during the first days

of El Celler de Can Roca, in 1986, to now working with 40 cooks in the kitchen. I learned that managing such a team in an inclusive way based on all their various talents depends on managing their abilities, creativities and emotions. The only way to do this was by actively listening. That's why on Tuesdays we decided not to have lunch service at the restaurant, rejecting the economic benefits of it, and keep this time for the team. Now we are able to have some time with them to share our projects and give them master-class training. We also decided to contract a Human Relations Psychologist expert, Imma Puig, who worked with FC Barcelona, to help take care of our staff and ourselves through group dynamics.

DAY IN, DAY OUT

We have achieved our present position by committing to hard work, creativity, our roots and authenticity. Luckily, success has knocked at our door, but we have followed no other strategy than commit-

ting to these ideas to get to this point. We live our cuisine day in and day out. I wake up a chef and I go to sleep a chef. This is the way it's been since I can remember.

REMARKABLE CONFIDENCE

We cook to awaken the senses and emotions. All of our work, research and creativity point to enhancing the guest experience in that direction. The most remarkable thing is the confidence that people give to us: they come to our restaurant open-hearted, ready to eat and drink what we offer to them using the ingredients we think are the best of the natural season in our land. We cook them in the best way we know how, with both respect and creativity. I'm also very lucky to have a brother that is considered one of the best sommeliers in the world, and he is very generous and sensitive to suggest a pairing to enhance each dish.

OUR PHILOSOPHY

Our creative process is a three-way collaboration, a synthesis of our three disciplines: Josep for wine, Jordi for sweet, and me for salt. Each of us provides our own vision for a new dish or a new project in every step we take. We start from 16 key concepts that define our philosophy from which we draw outwards. Some

of those starting points include product, landscape, academicism, memory, humor, boldness, innovation, perfume, poetry, magic, wine, and colorology. It is ultimately a sum of worlds coming together—a fluid dialogue with a common thread of passion, fun and rigor.

THE PERFECT DISH

A perfect dish is a dish cooked and served with love, and by this I mean love for cooking, love for the product in your hands, love for being a chef, love for your natural environment that gives you the ingredients, love for the people that are going to eat what you cook, and love for the team you are cooking with. Then, it must be eaten with love.

A SUSTAINABLE FUTURE

Future cuisine needs a healthy planet. If we don't take care of our planet, we will lose our natural pantry. Through our work as United Nations Development Programme ambassadors, we are committed to sustainability in our activities, collaborating with programs such as Food Africa in Kaduna, Nigeria, or taking local action to drive our restaurant operations to zero waste.

Jonnie Boer

BORN IN:

Giethoorn, The Netherlands

BASED IN:

Zwolle, The Netherlands

EXPERIENCE:

35 years

SELECT ACCOLADES:

De Librije | 97.50/100 in La Liste (2019)

De Librije | 3 Michelin Stars (2019)

De Librije | No. 51 on the World's 50 Best (2018)

Photo to the Left by Rahi Rezvani

"There is no magic bullet. You go through trial and error, over and over again, until your creation is perfect."

EARLY DAYS

I would characterize my early experiences in a professional kitchen as heavy but exciting. It was a real challenge in all aspects. It required a lot in terms of commitment and investment, but it was, and still is, a wonderful profession. Back in those days, gastronomy in The Netherlands nearly didn't exist. It was all about French cuisine. I always followed my own path and passion, and I never compromised on quality, and those are hallmark features of my culinary career to this day.

THE POWER OF PASSION

We always have applicants to our team on trial for a few days. Experience is not that important. What we look for are people with passion, perseverance and the right personality. I believe that people perform better when they are treated well, so I always stay calm, take everything step by step and maintain a birds-eye view. Yelling does not help any situation. The most important feature of a healthy team is communication, but in the end, it all comes back to loving what you do and the passion you have for this profession and the craft.

WE DON'T BELIEVE IN FAILURE

In 1993, the year we were awarded with our first Michelin star, we received a bad review. Back then the review was substantiated. It was a terrible feeling and we didn't sleep properly for a week. But it only made us more determined. We believed in what we were doing back then. Today, we learn to deal with critical feedback and put it in perspective.

In July of 2018 we celebrated our 25th anniversary. Those 25 years came with victories and setbacks, the most difficult of times being in 2008 after opening Librije's luxury hotel. We nearly went bankrupt. Our friends, family and team never lost trust or confidence in us. Together we fought hard to get back up and we couldn't have done it without them.

Photo by Thomas Ruhl

It's about trying and working hard. We don't believe in failure. While you may not succeed all the time, at least you gave it your all and learned along the way. These experiences made us stronger, both personally and professionally.

A CLEAR VIEW

Today, there isn't much that keeps me up at night. Thérèse and I are involved in every single aspect of De Librije. We know exactly what goes on. When you're involved in the details, both on the business side and the culinary side, you're able to maintain a clear view. We have a firm grasp of our finances, quality of products, expectations of guests and of our team, and of new developments in the kitchen. We are in close contact with our guests, too, listening to their feedback, and we have maintained our mantra of never compromising on quality.

WHAT DRIVES US

Our goal is doing what we love. We don't work in anticipation of awards or accolades of any kind. It is wonderful to be recognized for what we do, but that's not what drives us. We focus on our guests, not the awards. We maintain the quality and consistency of our offering by staying curious and experimenting with different products, regions, cultures, flavors and textures. There is no magic bullet. You go through trial and error, over and over again, until your creation is perfect.

CREATIVITY IN ALL FORMS

The most important feature of everything we do is creativity—not only in the kitchen, but in our whole operation. It's not only about being creative in your dishes, but also in management and hospitality. We listen to our guests and translate their feedback into business goals, all the while maintaining the Librije signature and essence. It has to be authentic.

The moment a guest arrives, they are immersed in the world of De Librije. They become part of the family to whom we share our passion and love. Both guests and staff feel that energy. Our creativity shows not only in our dishes, but also in exciting and different pairings—wine, tea, beer or some other new combination. More generally, as we are a luxury hotel too, we regularly renew the interior of the restaurant and hotel rooms to keep the ambiance fresh.

Photos to the Left and Right by Ron Greve

MIND TO PLATE

I think in terms of flavors and textures. In my head they all come together. Inspiration strikes at all times so I carry a little notebook with me where I scribble down the first thoughts in a drawing. Of course, it is then about creating, trial and error, and fine-tuning. A few times each year my team and I sit together to bring to life all of our new ideas. Some of them turn into complete disasters, but we always manage to discover new, exciting combinations. There is a lot you can learn during this process, but true creativity comes from within. We might create a dish that's not so great, but by adding one ingredient, or by removing one ingredient, it can transform the result into something spectacular.

For example, one of the combinations we never thought would be so fantastic was blue cheese and chocolate with Old Harvest Ximénez Spínola from Spain. Another dish I believe in very much is our crayfish and deconstructed apple pie. The apple pie is my mother's recipe, and when coupled with the crayfish, the flavors and textures are perfect.

THE PERFECT MOMENT

Creating the perfect dish is a struggle because perfection is intimately tied to a snapshot or a moment in time. You will want to create something new soon after and label that as perfect, too, so the notion of perfection is always changing and evolving. In other words, perfection is contextual. For me, perfection is not only creating the perfect dish. It is what happens when all aspects come together: food, wine, ambiance, service and a happy guest.

Photo to the Right by Ron Greve

José Andrés

BORN IN:

Mieres, Asturias, Spain

BASED IN:

Washington, DC, USA

EXPERIENCE:

33 years

SELECT ACCOLADES:

minibar | 86.25/100 in La Liste (2019)

minibar | 2 Michelin Stars (2019)

James Beard Humanitarian of the Year (2018)

> **"If you take a step back and look at an ingredient as if it were for the first time, you will always see something new."**

OPENED MY EYES

Early on I enlisted to be a cook in the Spanish Navy, at first for the Admiral, and then on a ship that sailed around the world. We went to the Ivory Coast, Brazil, the Caribbean, and America. It was seeing new places, meeting new people, and learning about cultures and cuisines that confirmed that this was what I wanted to be doing with my life. It was through cooking that I was able to see so many different places. It opened my eyes to the world.

A LEGENDARY MENTOR

After beginning to cook professionally, I met my first great mentor and friend, Ferran Adrià, the amazing chef at elBulli. I could see he was doing revolutionary things at his restaurant, even back then when we were both very young. He was always so creative, brilliant, and driven. I remember one night when I was working for him on the pastry section. It was cold and rainy. We did not think we would have any guests in the restaurant because of the weather. The pastry chef told Ferran that he didn't want to put together the pastry cart for service. Ferran said to us, "Today, I want to see the best dessert cart." He didn't care about wasting money. He wanted to keep us engaged, creative and committed.

HIRE PEOPLE SMARTER THAN YOU

I am always hiring people who are smarter than me—those who could be my boss. The other key to success is to flatten the organizational structure. Running a company as a pyramid, where messages from the very top get filtered down to all the people at the bottom is not an effective system. Instead, if there is an open line of communication all around the company, at the end of the day the best ideas will surface no matter who came up with them. This keeps the whole team engaged, excited, and motivated to be coming up with the next big thing. There is an old proverb that if you want to go fast, go alone. If you want to go far, go together. This is how I like to run my company, and how I live my life.

HISTORY FEEDS CREATIVITY

Creativity is everything, but it is always important to be very knowledgeable about what has come before. This is when creativity can truly blossom. Think about it: there have been so many amazing, creative, innovative chefs and cooks throughout all of history, so it doesn't make sense to be starting from scratch every day, pretending like nothing has come before. To be our most creative, we must travel, we must taste, we must meet other people and other chefs and understand what they are working

on and what inspires them, all before we ourselves can be inspired to come up with new things.

A FRESH PAIR OF EYES

I am looking for inspiration everywhere—every bite of food, every trip I take, every person I speak with can be a source of inspiration. I am constantly doing research. I brought my team to the most incredible farm in Ohio, the Chef's Garden, where my friend Farmer Lee Jones grows amazing vegetables and herbs. We toured the farm and filled up our arms with all of this fresh produce and then we went to the kitchen and experimented for two days. Carrots turned into pasta, into sauce, into curry, and into cocktails. Vegetable pulp became the base for fried rice. Beet juice was baked into cakes. If you take a step back and look at an ingredient as if it were the first time, you will always see something new.

NO MORE SALT ON THE RIM

Sometimes a new idea just hits me. One example is the salt air margarita, which we serve at Oyamel and in a few of my other restaurants. I love margaritas—the balance of sweet and sour and salty—but I have never liked the coarse salt on the rim. It can be so harsh. Then one day I was sitting on the beach with my wife Tichi in the south of Spain. We were watching the ocean's foamy waves crash onto the shore and I thought about how light and salty those waves would taste on my lips. And it hit me. No more salt on the rim. Just the salty sea foam, floating on top of the margarita. This "salt air" uses a sugar ester called sucro that creates an emulsification of liquid and air, as well as building up the surface tension to create a strong, stable foam. This foam can sit on top of the margarita and not melt

before you have a chance to drink it all. I promise it won't take you very long to drink the whole thing.

EVERY PLATE CAN BE IMPROVED

There can be very good, great, amazing, incredibly delicious dishes, but there is no such thing as the perfect dish. Every plate can always be improved so we must never get complacent and think that we have achieved perfection. There are many dishes that I have made hundreds if not thousands of times in my life. *Sopa de ajo*, Spanish garlic soup, is one that I had growing up with my family, and now I make it for my wife and daughters. I make it different every single time based on what we have in the house. Is each one good? Yes. Are any of them perfect? Of course not.

OPEN TO INTERPRETATION

There is no such thing as the perfect recipe. If you are writing down the recipe for caramelized onions, for example, what does it mean to say "take two onions, slice them, put them in a pan with olive

oil, and cook until caramelized." Every single one of those directions is open to interpretation. What kind of onions? How big are the slices? What size is the pan? How much heat does it transfer? What is the quality of the olive oil, and how much should you use? Each adjustment must be learned, not told, to really know how to cook. And that's why dishes will never be perfect. We can always be improving, perfecting our skills, and finding better ingredients.

THE POWER TO CHANGE THE WORLD

The best advice I can give new chefs is to not be afraid of failure. Being young and inexperienced is a great thing. You're able to have a new perspective on the world and not repeat the mistakes of the past. Learn as much as you can from history. And always remember that food is one of the most important things for humanity's survival, and it is central to global issues like poverty, the environment and immigration. Every day you are in the kitchen, think broadly about how powerful you are and about how important your skills are to the world.

José Avillez

BORN IN:

Lisbon, Portugal

BASED IN:

Lisbon, Portugal

EXPERIENCE:

14 years

SELECT ACCOLADES:

Belcanto | 90.25/100 in La Liste (2019)

Belcanto | 2 Michelin Stars (2019)

Belcanto | No. 75 on the World's 50 Best (2018)

Photo to the Left by Boa Onda

"I love to create. Nothing excites me more than the feeling of bringing to life that which exists only in the mind."

FOUND MY CALLING

I've had a passion for food since I was a child. To be more precise, it was really a passion for eating. I started cooking at home when I was seven. I used to bake with my sister, selling the cakes to family, friends and neighbors. We didn't measure the ingredients but the cakes came out fine. In my senior year of studying business communication, I decided to pursue my interest in becoming a chef.

In that same year, I participated in individual study sessions with Maria de Lourdes Modesto, the most important Portuguese author on traditional Portuguese cuisine—who encouraged me very much. I realized I had found my calling. I learned at the hand of Antoine Westermann at Fortaleza do Guincho, at Alain Ducasse's school, in Éric Frechon's kitchen at Le Bristol Paris, and at the renowned elBulli—a step that truly changed my career and my life.

THE SECRET

I have a very professional and passionate team. We work really hard, we trust our intuition, we listen very carefully to our clients, and we persevere. My main challenge is to ensure that everyone knows that they're an essential part of the team, irrespective of their function. I always try to find the right place for each person and to recognize the effort and commitment of each team member. Giving everyone clear direction and letting them know where we are headed is also very important. Most of all, it's vital that people have a stake in our collective success. That's the secret. I really believe I have the best team in the world. We are like an orchestra. Everyone knows what to do and when to do it.

Photo by Boa Onda

ALWAYS IMPROVING

There is a lot of pressure to maintain the standard, quality and consistency day in and day out, but I don't think about it. Our goal, since day one, has been to give our best, go further and surpass expectations. I'm very disciplined with myself and others, and I am constantly rethinking processes and finding ways to improve. Consistency comes from practice and from having a team who is as extraordinarily committed as I am.

A LARGER MISSION

Nothing of consequence can be achieved alone. I have a great team and I try to surround myself with people who are better than me in different areas. That's the only way we can do better because we learn from each other and grow together. There are difficult moments when I'm tired and don't feel like getting up in the morning having only slept two hours the night before, and having worked for twenty hours the previous day, but I love what I do.

I offer pleasurable moments to the people who sit at our table, have the opportunity to make a difference in the lives of the 550 people that work with us, and contribute to make Portugal's name and Portuguese gastronomy appreciated and known throughout the world.

Photo to the Left by Paulo Barata

NOTHING EXCITES ME MORE

Creativity is a complex process that's difficult to explain. I've always been curious and attentive. I'm a natural at recalling a great deal of memories and information. I travel whenever I can, and I'm always looking to learn through books, classes, people, movies and beyond. I always have new ideas, though sometimes not directly related to dishes and flavors, but about concepts, design and project development.

Whenever I go on a longer trip, I use that time to think. My team always gets very excited for my return home because they know I'll bring news and changes. Often times I text them during my travels so they can test this or that idea in real-time, or so they can make a change to a dish we serve. Then, when I get home, I confirm the results. By that point, the new dish is usually 90 percent complete. I love to create, and nothing excites more than the feeling of bringing to life that which exists only in the mind.

THE JOY OF SURPRISING

The drive to innovate comes from my passion for food and from the joy I feel by surprising others. My greatest inspiration comes from traditional Portuguese cuisine. Even though all of my restaurants have very different concepts, there's also a distinct Portuguese inspiration—more or less—in all of them.

Every time I'm abroad I visit the local markets, eat street food and explore the restaurant scene. That way I soak up everything I can about that particular country. Inspiration from my travels may take a while to reveal itself, but it can strike unexpectedly, like when I created the Vietnamese pork sandwich in Mini Bar or the lamb tagine with couscous in Cantinho do Avillez.

EVOLUTION

The notion of perfection is relative and subjective. My main goal is to offer pleasurable moments to the person eating. Every day we give all we've got to offer the best experience possible. However, I'm permanently trying to learn more and do better, and I try to instill this spirit in my team. In that sense, evolution is a very important word for me. It's no coincidence this word is the name of Belcanto's principal tasting menu.

WORD TO THE WISE

I would advise young and aspiring chefs to study as much as you can. Studying, even other areas, will broaden your horizon and teach you to be disciplined. And then if cuisine is truly what you're passionate about, you will have to work hard and never quit. To succeed in the world of cuisine, you have to be disciplined, committed and humble. You have to be willing to make a lot of sacrifices. It's not easy to start working in a kitchen, but the work does pay off. Above all, you must have an unwavering passion for food.

Photos to the Right by Paulo Barata

Kevin Fehling

BORN IN:

Delmenhorst, Germany

BASED IN:

Hamburg, Germany

EXPERIENCE:

24 years

SELECT ACCOLADES:

The Table | 95.25/100 in La Liste (2019)

The Table | 3 Michelin Stars (2018)

Photos to the Left by René Riis

"For me, creativity is linked to emotional intelligence, while manual labor is linked to rational intelligence. I'm very grateful to have more of the former."

SOMETHING EXTRAORDINARY

I've always been interested in the food industry. My mother, who often had three jobs at once, raised us two kids with the support of our father, and somehow always found time to cook fresh meals for us. At home we always had traditional, northern German cuisine prepared with love. What propelled me to become a chef was something else, though: I wanted to prove to myself and others that it's possible to do something extraordinary in life.

REACHED MY LIMITS

My first professional experience was in the Park Hotel Breman which, at the time, was one of Germany's grand hotels with a kitchen to match. The chef, Bernhard Stumpf, had an awful temper, but he also had a fascinating way of teaching me to value cooking by properly appreciating luxury products and their perfect preparation. I worked a split shift, meaning half a shift in the morning and half a shift in the evening. During the break I always sat in my apartment wondering whether I should go back that evening. Ultimately, I had a larger goal in mind that brought me back to the kitchen every night.

SOLO ENTREPRENEUR

The biggest challenge to leading a restaurant like The Table is to establish the restaurant economically. Most gourmet restaurants in the high-end segment generally only survive through an investor or are part of a luxury hotel. I'm a solo entrepreneur and have no investor or hotel as security. My main challenge is to follow through with the original business plan—to fill up the restaurant every day. For us to remain successful we must continuously evolve creatively, take very well care of our team, and win the monthly financial battle that comes with running a three Michelin star restaurant.

THE TRUE COST

We can do something extraordinary with the best salmon, for example, by giving the fish a certain taste through a particular cooking process. That means we do not simply hunt for luxury products. With our restaurant concept at The Table, we can calculate the cost of each meal perfectly because we only offer a fixed menu and cook for the same number of people every day. Therefore we always know what quantities have to be ordered and there

are no negative surprises in the evening. Many restaurateurs are reluctant to demand the true cost of the menu price, but you must in order to act economically.

TRUST YOUR INSTINCT

Since my cooking style is open-minded and modern, creativity plays a very big role in my life. The creative process is continuous and requires discipline. I sleep with it in the evening and wake up with it in the morning. The older I get, the more I realize that it doesn't always depend on a specific combination of flavors and textures, but rather a steady building of trust in my own creativity. For me, creativity is linked to emotional intelligence, while manual labor is linked to rational intelligence. I'm very grateful that I have more emotional intelligence than rational, which allows me to understand art, but I believe true artistic abilities cannot be learned.

MIND TO PLATE

When creating a new dish, we start off with an idea and then I draw multiple variants of that idea on paper. Often, a dish can be made of up to 15 different recipes that have been combined into one. The perfect arrangement, or visual presentation of the idea, and the choice of plates are also decided and created at this stage. The dish is then cooked and tested as long as it takes until I consider it perfect. When you decide to put a new dish on the menu, you must be 100 percent certain that it's even better than the one being replaced.

Photos to the Left and Right by René Riis

ON THE MENU

We continue to develop the classic combination of strawberry, rhubarb and almond, and every year we find a more perfect garnish to accompany a different protagonist—currently the scallop. We also have an eel that is prepared according to an ancient Japanese technique. It took me two years to perfect this dish. The fresh filet is first grilled, then cooked soft in water, soy sauce, mirin, rice vinegar and sugar, and glazed with a reduced fond and then grilled again.

A SCENT OF INSPIRATION

Inspiration for creating new dishes can come from anywhere. It could come from my daughter dropping a bottle of Marc Jacobs perfume into my wife's bath. That gave me the idea to put the taste and smell of that perfume on a plate, and also to build the architecture of the dish to look like that perfume bottle. Inspiration could also come from the traditional cooking of my mother, which has been ingrained in me since childhood. For example, at The Table we have done a modern interpretation of kale with cooked sausage, *pinkel* and cured pork.

LIMITLESS CREATIVITY

The whole planet is inspiring. I sailed across the sea in 2000 and 2002, and got to know the whole world. I've been inspired ever since. Limiting myself to a 50km or 100km radius for product selection means limiting myself creatively. For me, if you limit yourself physically, you limit yourself mentally.

THE NATURE OF PERFECTION

I don't think chefs can ever achieve perfection, since every three Michelin star cook has his or her own unique, signature style. Our profession is very subjective, so I don't think there can ever be a perfect dish, and yet we have this desire and passion to constantly seek perfection. I do believe there are perfect recipes, which takes us back to the rational side of manual labor. Creating the perfect dish is not a battle, but a goal.

THE FUTURE OF FOOD

I don't follow any trends since it's important for me to always set my own standards. More broadly, the progress of cooking techniques will be a little slower, since Ferran Adrià already set the standards for technique over 15 years ago, and was several years ahead of his contemporaries. Now and in the coming years, we will continue to profit from his wisdom. In addition, we must continually remind humanity that we do not have endless resources on this planet.

Photos to the Right Courtesy of The Table

Kwong Wai Keung

BORN IN:

Hong Kong SAR, China

BASED IN:

Hong Kong SAR, China

EXPERIENCE:

45 years

SELECT ACCOLADES:

T'ang Court | 91.25/100 in La Liste (2019)

T'ang Court | 3 Michelin Stars (2019)

All Photos Courtesy of T'ang Court

> **"One day I was attracted to a brief aroma of stir-fried black beans, which inspired me to create a dish so fragrant than it can be smelled by diners before they see it."**

JOB TO CAREER

I entered the culinary industry as a teenager to merely earn an income, but soon after I matured, realizing my passion for cooking. It was enormously satisfying working in the kitchen and from that point on, I believed being a chef would be my life-long career.

WATCH CLOSELY

When I first joined the industry, executive chefs in Chinese kitchens would not actively teach junior chefs. Observation was the key to learning in a Chinese kitchen. You would have to memorize how the executive chefs cooked all of the dishes, and master these skills by trial and error. Today, I always step into the shoes of my junior staff to understand their wants, needs and ambitions. I observe their abilities and potential from day one, and when the time comes, I empower them to embrace new opportunities to upgrade their skills and advance professionally.

THE FUNDAMENTALS

The foundation of every successful dish is rooted in the quality of ingredients. Over the years, I've studied different types of products to figure out which cooking techniques best bring out the flavors and textures of each dish. I have also spent much time leading our efforts to source the best ingredients we can. Simply put, my philosophy is to cook whole-heartedly and maintain the integrity of the products.

KEY TO SUCCESS

Good communication, mutual trust and respect are the hallmarks of how the team at T'ang Court works together. Indeed, teamwork is critical to success. I have worked with our Director of Operations at the restaurant, Mr. Danny Chan, for almost 30 years. His support and leadership is essential to making T'ang Court one of the top Cantonese restaurants in the world.

HARNESS THE SENSES

Most of my cooking inspiration comes from daily life. For example, one day I was attracted to a brief aroma of stir-fried black beans, which inspired me to create a dish so fragrant than it can be smelled by diners before they see it. The dish, which won an accolade at the Hong Kong Tourism Board's culinary awards, was stir-fried fresh lobster with spring onion, red onions and shallots. After 45 years as a chef, I believe I have mastered the process of creating a new dish. Of course, there are times when some ideas don't turn out as perfectly as expected, but often after investigating the root cause of the issue, the quality of the product could have been better sourced. This is why I always emphasize the sourcing of ingredients as one of the most important aspects of creating the perfect dish.

THE RIGHT BALANCE

T'ang Court specializes in presenting very traditional Cantonese cuisine, so when we think about

perfection, the perfect dish is one that upholds and brings out the best flavors and textures of the ingredients, while also staying true to authentic Cantonese tradition. While I always keep an eye on the newest ingredients and cooking equipment on the market, the most important thing is to match the appropriate cooking technique with the ingredient at hand. If I discover that there are ways to improve any of our dishes to a great extent, it's time for that dish to evolve.

A VALUABLE TREASURE

Today's diners are getting more and more exposure to various types of cuisines from around the world, from local street foods to fine dining, and they are more knowledgeable than ever about culinary dis-

tinctiveness. Looking ahead, I believe traditional Cantonese cuisine will be better understood as a unique and valuable treasure of Cantonese heritage.

A HEALTHY FUTURE

As diners are more health conscious, we must not only be careful in our selection of ingredients, but we must also strike the right balance between meat and vegetables in any given dish. Moreover, I always emphasize the importance of food safety in relation to the health of our diners. Low quality ingredients, MSG and other additives are being used to enhance dishes—despite their adverse impacts—so we must always put this issue in the spotlight.

Martha Ortiz

BORN IN:

Mexico City, Mexico

BASED IN:

Mexico City, Mexico

EXPERIENCE:

18 years

SELECT ACCOLADES:

Dulce Patria | 96.75/100 in La Liste (2019)

Dulce Patria | No. 48 on Latin America's 50 Best (2017)

Photo to the Left by Pepe Molino
All Other Photos by Jean Cazals

"My daily mantra is the thirst for justice and the hunger for beauty."

RECREATING MEMORIES

My mother, who was an artist and a great cook, always had the ability to extract and create beauty from food and took great pleasure in doing so. She created dishes that were inspired by all kinds of experiences, and that were full of textures, scents, colors and flavors. Observing her every move inspired a lifelong passion, and I realize as a chef today that I am recreating all of those wonderful memories and interactions between colors, flavors, art and the blessings of being a woman. Above all, I learned early on that passion is the most important ingredient, seasoning life and everything our gastronomic vision produces.

INSPIRED BY MATISSE

When I was in high school, I went to a legendary restaurant in New York City called the Quilted Giraffe. It has since closed, but the plates were adorned with sauces that looked like Matisse's brush strokes. It was both unique and inspiring, like being at a museum.

JUSTICE AND BEAUTY

As a woman, I am interested in empowering other women, which is complicated in a country like Mexico, which has very few inclusive policies. I learned that the kitchen is a place for freedom, and that it is important to recognize that and highlight women's labor. As a women, it is very easy to fall to the temptation of imitating male cooks in their attitude and style. Not succumbing to this temptation necessitates believing in yourself, having confidence and being connected with the aesthetics of female chefs. My daily mantra is the thirst for justice and the hunger for beauty.

FEEDING THE SOUL

You must think of nourishment as something beyond food. You must feed yourself by absorbing and learning about other disciplines in order to ignite the imagination. I visit museums, delight in music and opera, read literature and poetry, and respect the texture of painting techniques. It is there, in the artistic ability of others, where I feel inspired and motivated to create.

THE PERFECT DISH

Creativity, along with fantasy and imagination, plays a fundamental role in my life as a chef. But it must also be understood that creativity without consistency does not go far. You must be disciplined in your efforts. Creativity becomes a vessel for us to deliver the flavors of our food. I don't believe the perfect dish exists, but as chefs, part of our craft is striving for perfection hoping to create a masterpiece.

GASTRONOMIC EVOLUTION

The structure of some dishes must never change. For example, I will never take an ingredient out of a *mole*, for it is the perfect witchcraft that has been devised over many years. When the structure and preparation allows for a dish to evolve, it is important that the original flavors stay intact. Mexican cuisine allows for something traditional to be updated with more modern techniques, aesthetics and beauty, for this notion reflects the nature of gastronomic evolution.

A COMPELLING STORY

I create a *libretto* to accompany each and every dish. It is essentially a compelling story of emotions, characters, ideas and a different approach to food. Specific words correspond with colors and tastes in the dish. Based on this story, I create small drawings, then go through the markets, museums and antique shops to find the perfect objects and flavors to bring this story to life. I keep a little notebook where I write and collect these stories, with many sketches of plates drawn with strokes of burned cinnamon. I circle back to these ideas that then become the guiding thread to my narrative and edible drama.

THE FUTURE OF FOOD

Looking ahead, gastronomy will be a more professionalized and profound vocation. There will be more historic, philosophical and artistic contexts, and it will not only be an ephemeral experience about immediate satisfaction. Advances in science and technology, including artificial intelligence and robotics, will have an impact on the profession of cooking. Ethics, too, will be important in terms of sourcing ingredients, animal cruelty, equality and social justice. There will also be an increased importance and emphasis on regional and seasonal ingredients, and solidarity with the countryside communities in sustainability and support.

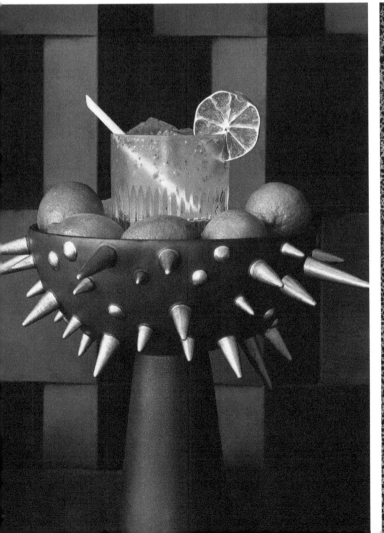

Martin Berasategui

BORN IN:

San Sebastián, Spain

BASED IN:

Lasarte-Oria, Spain

EXPERIENCE:

44 years

SELECT ACCOLADES:

Martin Berasategui | 99.50/100 in La Liste (2019)

Martin Berasategui | 3 Michelin Stars (2019)

Restaurante Lasarte | 3 Michelin Stars (2018)

All Photos by Jose Luis Lopez de Zubiria

"The most important book that has ever been written is the book of nature, and it's our responsibility to read it every morning."

A DIFFERENT TIME

My parents owned Bodegón Alejandro, which was considered an institution at the time. After school I would go to the restaurant, which was divided into two dining rooms: one for everyone and the other for family and close friends. The latter was the center of our lives. We only went home to sleep and bathe. There we played, listened to our elders and learned what life is all about. It was my own private university because the finest part of popular Basque society gathered there.

My father was a butcher by trade, and everyone knew him. Our tables were always packed with singers, poets, journalists, artists, sculptors, soccer players, reformists, boxers, fishermen, bakers, students, high school teachers and of course, other butchers. They would dine on a plate of chorizo or baked meat, a potato tortilla, steak, fish or whatever my mother and aunt made that day. I remember the atmosphere there between 1965 and 1975 with great nostalgia, as I realize now that it would be impossible to gather such an eclectic group of personalities in a similar fashion today.

AN OBSESSION

The most important thing I learned while studying with French pastry chefs is that they don't improvise. Everything is well-measured and calculated. Once you decide on making a cake or a pie, you experiment with the recipe, but when you find what you're looking for, you must write down the grams and the preparation. It's true that cooking is more of an intuitive nature, but this training has helped me a lot. I write down everything obsessively and I have an endless number of notebooks where I look up recipes and train my team so they know exactly what I want to make.

THE ESSENCE OF A CHEF

In our 350 square foot test room, we keep meticulous track of every new recipe—each of which has a detailed step by step process. We have a lot of recipes, as I've been at this for more than 40 years. Ultimately, the better dishes you make, the more satisfied you are. When a friend comes over to eat at my black marble kitchen table, I will know right away whether I've done well or not. If they're happy

with what I offered them, it makes me happy. That's my life. That's my goal and my point of view on this profession.

A MOMENT IN TIME

I don't settle with repeating what I did last year, no matter how proud I feel about it. Whether someone travels to eat at my restaurant from another corner of the world, or a young couple comes in with their savings to have a feast, I like to offer them what I am in this moment, and not what I was a few years ago. My food is a mirror of what I feel at that moment in time.

THE BOOK OF NATURE

I am inspired by much in the world: an outing to the sea, a trip by plane, chatting with friends or reading a book. Creativity, however, is not simply brainstorming. You must work on your ideas for them to have creative value. Originality must be justified, otherwise it's worthless. The most important book that has ever been written is the book of nature. It's our responsibility to read it every morning as soon as we wake up. Nature is an endless source of inspiration from which you can translate into emotions. We chefs try to turn these emotions into gastronomic creations.

EXTRAORDINARY RAW MATERIALS

The first thing a chef must look after is raw material. I demand that my vegetables are of excellent quality. I take extraordinary measures to ensure this and have specialized people that bring me what I ask for. I no longer go to the markets,

but instead the providers themselves are the ones that fill our pantry. For instance, I source soft peas, barnacles, mushrooms, oysters, and other products even before they reach the local market. My restaurant is not a common one: people come to eat extraordinary things, and to do so you need extraordinary raw materials.

THE CREATIVE PROCESS

While there isn't a fixed rule on how best to create, I do have my method. When I have an idea, I think about the materials and possible combinations. I write it down in a notebook and test it in our creative room at my restaurant. If I like it, it gets passed on to my head chefs and they fine-tune it. Then I put together the technology and the human factor, so it can be reproduced in all my restaurants

in the same way because it needs to be consistently perfect every time.

Overall, we focus on technique, cooking point, the cut, textures, selection, freshness of the raw materials, the harmony of the full menu, the ration, temperature and even the tempo. Everything is important. Usually, if a new dish amazes me, the diners are amazed too, because if you can say anything at all about chefs, it's that their palates are highly developed.

THE PERFECT DISH

All of my latest creations at my restaurants are perfect dishes. I wouldn't allow myself to offer dishes that are not perfect per my palate. I always try to make sure that my newest dishes be, at mini-

135

mum, as good or better than the previous ones. My menu includes some perfectly prepared traditional dishes, which my customers would never let me remove, along with some highly innovative creations. The truth is that the higher the standard, the more demanding you become, and perfection becomes more and more difficult. Therefore, our creative testing room is essential so that we can be innovating all year long.

CAREER WISDOM

For new and aspiring chefs, you must work with passion and discipline, because those are the two fundamental ingredients that any good chef needs to pursue their dreams. If you really want to devote yourself to cooking, fight without throwing in the towel, even if times are hard, because perseverance and tenacity are fundamental to success. I would also advise you to be patient, humble and honest. Goals are achieved little by little, which is something young people, because of their natural rush, sometimes fail to comprehend.

DAY IN THE LIFE

My daily routine is quite simple. I wake up very early, usually at the break of dawn, and go for a walk. I like to do this before each working day as it helps me focus. By 9:30AM, I am ready with my kitchen team to organize the day's work. We brainstorm new ideas at our creative test bench and deal with other issues that crop up. This is a daily routine that goes past midnight, when we finally have the kitchen spotless and ready for the next day. I have always seen my profession as one of absolute dedication and passion. There's nothing more to it.

Matthew Orlando

BORN IN:

San Diego, CA, USA

BASED IN:

Copenhagen, Denmark

EXPERIENCE:

27 years

SELECT ACCOLADES:

Amass | Sustainable Restaurant of the Year by The White Guide (2017)

Photo to the Left by Mikkel Heriba
All Other Photos by Chris Tonnesen

"The ultimate satisfaction is when you taste a new flavor for which you have no reference, like tasting ice cream for the first time."

FOOD AND PEOPLE

When I was young we always had a garden. My parents would not only grow food, but they were also extremely open in having people over for dinner or a barbeque. At the time, I didn't realize how much this would affect my frame of mind, but this relationship between food and people has really shaped the way in which I approach the culinary profession: arms wide open.

ON TOP OF THE WORLD

My first job in the industry was at a pizza place when I was 14 years old. To this day it was the best pizza I've ever had. The coolest person in the kitchen was the one who got to make the pizza. I worked my tail off to get that role and at 15, when I finally achieved it, I was on top of the world.

LEAD BY EXAMPLE

As a leader, you need to be more motivated than your team. That means even when you're stressed or burned out, the staff can't see that. You set the mood both in and out of the kitchen, and for your guests to have the best experience possible, the mood needs to be energetic and inspiring. Leading by example is the best form of motivation. Because I set the tone at the top, I would never ask my staff to do something that I wouldn't do myself. I also learned that you must surround yourself with passionate people that really care about their work, and in that sense, I hire based on personality more than I do skill.

CREATIVE LOGIC

We have a saying at Amass: we'll try anything twice. This simply means that everyone has a chance to put their ideas into play. If they work that's amazing and if not, we go back to how we were doing things before. If you don't take chances, you'll never find new and inventive ways of doing things. With that said, a chef must never try and learn new techniques without mastering those of tradition. Without a historical understanding, you have no reference point, and without a reference point, you have no direction.

CALCULATED RISK

The biggest challenge to leading a renowned restaurant is balancing consistency with innovation. Generally, these two do not go hand in hand, but if you want a progressive restaurant, you have to innovate, and innovating means taking chances and compromising consistency. In other words, we compromise consistency in exchange for innovation. Of course, we do not simply shoot from the hip. To be confident in what you're serving, no matter how inventive, you must have a certain amount of experience.

But in the end, we have incorporated innovation as a rule, rather than as an exception. We never repeat a dish once it comes off the menu. We inform our guests of this and it becomes part of the experience. In fact, they are even more excited about eating a dish that will never be served again.

EMBRACE FAILURE

When trying new things, we have an 80 percent failure rate. You cannot be afraid of failure. Failure

means learning and learning means progression. I embrace failure and criticism. There is always something to be learned from both. You just need to develop a thick skin to take advantage of those moments.

LIFE OF A CHEF-OWNER

Money keeps me up at night. It's the most draining part of being a chef-owner. Profit margins at this level of restaurant are tight, and we must wear many different hats. For me, creativity is a release from the daily running of a restaurant. But as necessary as it is, you don't always have the mental space for it when you are the owner so you need a strong creative team around you to continue pushing boundaries.

THE ULTIMATE SATISFACTION

While texture directly effects flavor and how things move around your mouth and hit different taste buds, flavor is based on the season—what our brains and bodies should be craving at that particular time of year based on where you are in the world. Flavors inspire me to push limits. The ultimate satisfaction is when you taste a new flavor for which you have no reference. When you can stand there with your team and just smile because you all feel like little children tasting ice cream for the first time.

CREATIVITY IN REVERSE

We have a very sustainable profile as a restaurant and this affects our creativity. We put all of our different trim through processes to extract flavors that

are locked away. We do this through different types of fermentation, pickling, drying and other methods. By working this way, we have cut our waste going to the landfill by 75 percent. Creatively, we now start with our by-products and work backwards. The perfect piece of fish is the last component to hit the plate. Another influential part of the creative process is our 900 square meter garden overlooking the harbor. If you're in search of that final activator on a dish, I'm certain that if you take a walk through the garden and taste everything, you'll find it.

IN THE MOMENT

A dish could be tested for weeks or it could be plated for the first time in service. We don't restrict ourselves to one methodical way of being creative. The best dishes are created in the moment. What's more inspiring than 5kg of chanterelle mushrooms, picked 30 minutes ago, coming through the backdoor in the middle of service? If you restrict yourself to process and protocol, then you miss out on amazing opportunities to be creative.

THE SOUL OF A RESTAURANT

There is no such thing as the perfect dish. Taste is simply subjective. You need to accept the fact that you will never make 100 percent of your guests happy. If you do, then you are playing it safe and not evolving. If you don't evolve then the soul of your restaurant dies. Therefore, there is no such thing as perfection, only the pursuit of it. Imperfection is necessary to nurture evolution. Sometimes you need to let go of a dish or an idea that you are completely satisfied with in order to create something better.

A SUSTAINABLE FUTURE

We need to look at the whole product and not just the center cuts. I think sustainable restaurants are the only way forward. As a whole, the industry is cooking in a very irresponsible manner. We need to start being proactive and not reactive to the environmental challenges around us. New techniques to process by-products will be even more necessary to keep costs down. We need to embrace this evolution and look at this opportunity as a chance to discover new flavors. I urge chefs to get their restaurants' carbon footprint evaluated because I think it would be a rude awakening. When we had ours done some years ago, it changed my whole approach to running a restaurant.

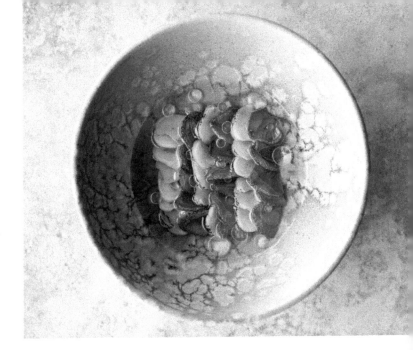

Nicolai Nørregaard

BORN IN:

Svaneke, Bornholm, Denmark

BASED IN:

Copenhagen, Denmark

EXPERIENCE:

20 years

SELECT ACCOLADES:

Kadeau | 85.50/100 in La Liste (2019)

Kadeau | 2 Michelin Stars (2018)

All Photos by Marie Louise Munkegaard

> **"I'm always searching for new techniques, new products, new flavors and new ways of preserving the seasons. The hunt for the new is an excellent motivator for me."**

A FAMILY OF TEACHERS

My great grandfather had his own butcher shop and was very passionate about food. He passed this passion onto my grandfather, who is the biggest influence of my culinary life. He was always in the kitchen cooking traditional dishes, but also refining them and trying to make them a little bit better. He looked to me to be able to tell the smallest differences in flavors, making even the simplest of dishes taste fantastic and complex. He made his own fermented herrings, grew his own vegetables, and preserved for the winter season.

My uncle was also in the industry, owning a legendary smokehouse called Kowsky's where I would spend a lot of time as a kid, learning the importance and precision of technique. Growing up in a self-supplying biodynamic collective with my mom and stepdad, who lived as vegetarians, gave me insight into a completely different way of living and producing vegetables. Although back then I thought it was odd, today I am grateful to have this experience in my backpack.

HUMBLE BEGINNINGS

I started out as a bellboy at a fancy hotel in Copenhagen—Hotel D'Angleterre—far away from the kitchen but still close enough to be intrigued by the buzz. On the other hand, I saw the craziness that ruled in the kitchen: shouting and screaming on a daily basis with pots and pans flying around. I then moved to work as a waiter in various restaurants and gradually started doing a little bit of cooking on the side. The first time I worked in a real kitchen was when we opened Kadeau. We hired a head chef so he could teach me the basics of running a professional kitchen. Slowly, I took over.

WHAT BINDS US TOGETHER

The key word underpinning our philosophy at Kadeau is family. We've always viewed our staff as family, and work hard to create an environment where our employees feel comfortable and secure. It's vital that staff love their work. There is no shouting or bullying. It is simply not accepted. Every summer we close Kadeau Copenhagen and

145

bring the whole staff to Bornholm island to work the high season there. We have a farmhouse where everyone lives together, like one big working-hol-iday-camp.

PERFECTING THE BALANCE

There is a thin line between success and failure in this business. For me, the most important feature is honesty. We must be completely honest about what we do, why we do it and how we do it. There's always talk about Michelin stars and lists of recog-nition, and I wish none of this was important, but I also admit that it is.

Deep down, I just want to be able to cook what I feel like cooking and make our guests happy, but at the end of the day, I know that being present in the media matters, that Michelin stars are extremely important for the business, and that recognition in certain lists drives full houses every day. What keeps me up at night is how to find the perfect bal-ance: financial success, recognition, Michelin stars, and the freedom of cooking with the heart.

FAILING TO SUCCEED

If something fails, or if I get criticized, it usually gets under my skin and affects me quite a lot. But in the end, it also works as fuel. It sparks motivation and determination to do things better or to try harder not to fail. In a way, I feel as though I need failure or setbacks to stay motivated and ambitious. You need to know what winter feels like to fully enjoy a summer day. It is the same with failure and success.

THE WAVE OF CREATIVITY

I thought I would end up as an architect, a designer or an artist. But I ended up in the kitchen with food as the media of my creative expression. I don't have a creative process. Sometimes creativity comes in small flashes before the inner eye, and sometimes it happens on the cutting board. Sometimes a dish is transformed from thought to plate exactly how it was conceived, and other times the idea of a dish vanishes in the process of testing it, ending up in a completely different direction. I believe real creativity comes from within, like a wave that can't be held back.

THE HUNT

I often seek inspiration in history and traditions. I'm always searching for new techniques, new products, new flavors and new ways of preserving the seasons. I'm always on the lookout for a new wild flower, cone or tree. The hunt for the new is an excellent motivator for me. It keeps me curious and adds an almost play-like dimension to my work. In fact, I just need to take a bike ride through the forest to come up with new ideas. That's the easy part. The difficult part is transforming that idea into a dish that makes it onto the menu.

A RARE EXCEPTION

Sometimes your ability to be creative surprises you. I once made a dish of raw scallop, cream, horseradish, reduced and dried mussel stock, hemp oil, scots pine and scallop *bottarga*. I had the dish perfectly conceived in my mind, and when I made the first test, it was spot on. But that is a very rare experience. Usually a dish changes direction, radically, once we begin testing. That process is extremely inspiring.

ON PERFECTION

There is no such thing as the perfect dish. There is the perfect balance, perfect temperature, and perfect technique, but a dish is never perfect because of variations in climate, season and environment. A dish is cooked hundreds and hundreds of times and will always be a little different from the last time. It's both ever-changing and ever-charming.

A NOBLE PROFESSION

My advice to young and aspiring chefs is that the culinary craft is one of the greatest in the world. It suits creative minds and the hands of craftsmen. Cooking for another human being is one of the most noble things you can do. It's so basic and yet so magnificent. But be aware, it's a very stressful and demanding profession. It's long hours and weekends away from friends and family, but it's definitely worth it.

THE FUTURE OF FOOD

In terms of gastronomic trends, I think we will see a more unified world kitchen. I don't think we'll see a great world-changing gastronomical epiphany any time soon. The Nordic movement was the last great revolution. Today every kitchen has a little of that in it. We now see Asian influences in the north and African influences in the South. The next great kitchen is a world kitchen, varied by the products available to the time and place each of us finds ourselves in. The future of food is both global and hyper-local.

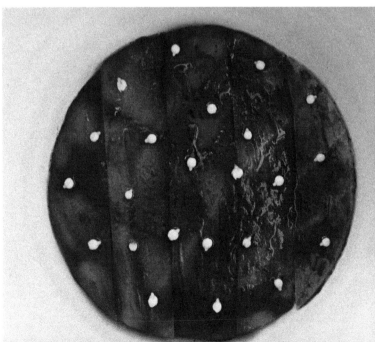

Niki Nakayama

BORN IN:

Los Angeles, CA, USA

BASED IN:

Los Angeles, CA, USA

EXPERIENCE:

22 years

SELECT ACCOLADES:

n/naka | 80.00/100 in La Liste (2019)

n/naka | Eater's 38 Essential Restaurants in America (2019)

n/naka | Los Angeles Times 101 Best Restaurants (2018)

Photo to the Left by Katrina Dickson
All Other Photos Courtesy of n/naka

"The biggest hindrance to creativity and inspiration is trying to control or manipulate the process."

THE BEGINNING

Since I was very young, eating and cooking has always brought people together and was always part of something celebratory. I started to consider a culinary career when I lived in Japan for one year after high school. But after spending a summer at my relative's *ryokan* in Japan's countryside, I knew that it was something I wanted to pursue. When I returned to the United States I enrolled in culinary school.

When I first entered the industry, it was exciting and motivating. I loved the fast pace, the constant learning and the feeling of doing so many things with a limited amount of time.

COLLECTIVE SUCCESS

I'm a firm believer in the power of surrounding yourself with like-minded individuals because I've realized that we must all be on the same page with respect to our vision and what we want to achieve. One of the most important ways to maintain enthusiasm and motivation on the team is to ensure we all feel as though we are growing together both personally and professionally. We must all feel that we are better people today than we were yesterday.

MAINTAINING A BALANCE

While the biggest challenge we face is to continually improve and grow so that we are able to meet, if not exceed, expectations, what keeps me up at night is balancing the likes and needs of our guests without sacrificing our intentions in the work that we do. On some level, the work we do is personal and creative, but we also must remember that we are in the business of hospitality, where the experience and opinions of guests also deserve a voice. In the end, and above all, we always keep our eyes focused on the guest experience.

DELICIOUSNESS OVER CONCEPT

The creative process is something that happens only when you have a good handle on the technique, history and understanding of the craft. I understand that many people enjoy the creative aspects of what we do, but it is important to have the discipline in trying to master the technical aspects of the craft first so that your expression flows easily. After doing this for so many years, it's a lot easier to imagine flavors and textures together before creating such combinations in the kitchen. Sometimes a dish will magically come together without much effort, and other times it takes a lot

to make it work. I always feel that the dishes that come easily are truly the best dishes.

For example, the abalone pasta, which is a customer favorite, is the one dish that stays on our menu. Dishes that comfort or are just plain delicious are the ones that flow organically. If we're trying to create something with a visual wow factor, those take more planning and preparation, but we cannot sacrifice a wonderful ingredient to our desires of presentation. I always tell myself that above and beyond anything else, deliciousness over concept.

CREATIVE EXPRESSION

Creativity can be both taught and innate. I think on some level we can all be creative, but it takes a mastery of the craft to be able to express that cre-

ativity in a meaningful way. You must know how to bring that creativity to life into something tangible for it to be experienced. Therein lies the art of being truly creative.

SOURCES OF INSPIRATION

Inspiration is everywhere, be it books, research, or photographs, but I must be in the right frame of mind to see it and feel it. I think it comes more naturally when my mind is relaxed and not stressed. Often I am most inspired with an "a-ha" moment when not doing anything at all related to cooking, like taking a shower. However, sometimes if I'm under extreme pressure, I am also able to become inspired. Both situations are nonetheless conducive to creativity. I find that the biggest hindrance to creativity and inspiration is trying to control or manipulate the process.

MIND TO PLATE

When creating a new dish, I usually start with ingredients that I'd like to work with and try to recall how I've enjoyed them. I then think about the traditional ways in which they are usually prepared and other flavors that would enhance those original ingredients. I also try to think of new and interesting ways to present their essence. From there, it's a matter of trial and error in the kitchen. It's a process of discovery that's never fully planned or imagined. It's a flow that leads from one moment to the next, making it up as I go along. After I feel that all the elements work together, I'll begin the plating process.

For example, I wanted to create a dish using sea urchin that was encapsulated by a *uni* chocolate shell. In my mind, I envisioned something along the lines of the textures of a chocolate truffle, but it being savory with the flavors of sea urchin. It took a little bit of research into what kinds of ingredients we could use to make it happen, and after some trial and error, it came to life. On the other hand, I once had an idea of pairing sea urchin with corn, thinking it would go well together because of their sweetness and mild flavors, only to discover that the pairing didn't work.

KNIFE SKILLS

First and foremost, the quality of ingredients is the most important piece of any dish. For sashimi, it's important to honor the pure flavor of the fish, so instead of doing very much to the product, it comes down to knife skills.

Patrick O'Connell

BORN IN:

Washington, DC, USA

BASED IN:

Washington, VA, USA

EXPERIENCE:

57 years

SELECT ACCOLADES:

The Inn at Little Washington |
98.75/100 in La Liste (2019)

The Inn at Little Washington |
3 Michelin Stars (2019)

All Photos Courtesy of Inn at Little Washington

"In its highest sense, I regard my work as a healing art form."

ABSURDITIES OF LIFE

My first job was in a restaurant at the impressionable age of 15. Once I discovered the intensity of this delicious business, I was hooked. More than anything, I fell in love with restaurant people. They all seemed to have a whacked sense of humor and a genuine appreciation for the absurdities of life.

Every day I felt like I was watching a split-screen film with two shows running simultaneously—the fantasy taking place in the dining room juxtaposed with what was going on behind the scenes in the rough and tumble world of the kitchen. I've never been bored for a minute in a restaurant kitchen. I love getting into "the zone" and forgetting I have a body or any problems. Every night I still find the addictive adrenaline rush exhilarating.

VERY MUCH LIKE AN ORCHESTRA

The team is united around a common goal of excellence without compromise. For me the key word is collaboration. Everyone's contribution is important and everyone has to be on cue. It's very much like an orchestra and my role is parallel to a conductor's. I'm always looking for any flaws and imperfections in our performance. It's important to understand how unforgiving a guest can be if something isn't as it should be. My role is to be our worst critic and to see the experience as a critical guest would view it.

GROWING OR DYING

One of the biggest challenges any restaurateur faces these days is the need to constantly re-invent themselves while still maintaining continuity and consistency. On each visit there needs to be a fresh surprise for the guest. An artist's work must reflect his or her taste at any given moment or it will register as inauthentic or stale. If a chef is bored with a dish it will be felt by the guest.

Our approach is simply to try to make everything a little bit better than it was the day before. Even the tiniest, incremental improvement brings a sense of satisfaction and is noticed by guests. Most importantly, it helps create a culture of upward ascendancy. The old adage that a restaurant is either growing or dying is deadly accurate. Standing still is dying.

YOU NEVER ARRIVE IN OUR BUSINESS

I often say that creativity can't be taught, it has to be caught. Getting in touch with ones innate sense of creativity is often an unlearning process rather than a learning one. There is no formula. You might have to embrace the opposite of what you were told would work. When you're nimble and open enough to follow an uncharted path it often leads you to a more original solution. Many great dishes have been concocted based on accidents and mistakes. Improvisation can often be freeing and a way to

155

get in touch with your unconscious creativity. Everything can always be improved. You never arrive in our business. After 40 years, I still say that we're about 60 percent of the way there.

JUST IMAGINE

I have to eat here every night and I get bored quickly. The young cooks get to experiment on me by cooking my dinner. I critique their dishes and give them feedback. More often than not that begins a dialogue and an exchange of ideas.

Since our menu is continually evolving, we sometimes choose a dish on the current menu that best exemplifies our direction and ask ourselves how the other dishes measure up. If they don't, we target them for replacement and someone begins working on a new alternative. The process usually takes weeks of critical tasting and evaluating to finally find its way on the menu. We sometimes bring back a dish we did 30 years ago, update it and breathe new life into it. Imagine the number of dishes we've created in more than 40 years with an ever-evolving seasonal menu.

IT WAS REBORN

For more than 25 years we've had a seared lamb carpaccio on the menu. Originally it was garnished with a little mound of tabouli in an era when few people knew what tabouli was. Then one day, it just felt tired. We eliminated the tabouli and inserted a garnish of caesar salad ice cream. It was an overnight sensation and gave new life to the dish. Eating it became an adventure. Everyone loved it. It was reborn. Sometimes we do a new take on a classic preparation such as our duck a l'orange reincarnat-

ed, eliminating everything heavy and out of fashion but keeping the essential essence and flavor profile.

WHOSE IDEA WAS THAT?

Sometimes a dish falls together spontaneously, but more often than not it's a long process of working with the germ of an idea and refining it. Once conceptualized, It takes about one month for a dish to get ironed out and perfected.

Everyone in the kitchen is invited to put a dish in front of me at any time for feedback. Usually there is an element of originality or a feature which might trigger another idea and it's often like a ping pong game. This is one of my favorite interactions with the team. It involves tapping into a collective con-sciousness. Sometimes it's impossible to remember whose idea was whose. The end result is a hybrid and much better than any one person could have conceived on their own. This process requires everyone to be non-competitive and non-judgmental in order for it to work.

THE IMPORTANCE OF TRADITION

There is too little appreciation for quality, excellence, and tradition. My hope is that we don't feel we have to throw away tradition entirely in order to embrace what's new. One of the ways in which we can increase the appreciation for tradition is by educating food journalists and critics. Few of them have the international reference points necessary to formulate an historical perspective.

A HEALING ART FORM

For the past 40 years, I've been attempting to combine the disciplines of theatre, the culinary arts and psychology in the creation of a unique restorative sanctuary—a stage set for a magical interlude out of time and place where worldly cares can be suspended, our faith in humanity restored, and the art of living celebrated.

WORDS OF WISDOM

My advice to young and aspiring chefs would be to become a voracious reader of restaurant reviews. Study the critics. Go to the best restaurants in your region and then in the world. Create reference points and benchmarks for yourself. Choose a chef and restaurant as a model of what you might wish to ultimately become. If you want to open a burger joint, don't aim for the best hamburger in town or your state—go for the best hamburger in the world. Find a mentor and a critic, preferably someone who has a world view and who will be brutally honest with you.

Pedro Subijana

BORN IN:

San Sebastián, Spain

BASED IN:

San Sebastián, Spain

EXPERIENCE:

50 years

SELECT ACCOLADES:

Akelarre | 96.25/100 in La Liste (2019)

Akelarre | 3 Michelin Stars (2019)

All Photos Courtesy of Akelarre

> **"Picasso once said that inspiration will find you while working, but I believe it can also find you while sleeping."**

THE BEST GRADES

Growing up, the ritual of cooking and serving food was considered very important. My father was a baker, and my grandfather took us to the best restaurants on both sides of the border. When I was 12 years old I burnt myself, secretly cooking in the kitchen because they would not let me, but at that point I never thought about becoming a cook. It was not considered a possibility after high school. In fact, I was going to become a doctor. But during the summer months before going to university, I decided to enroll in a catering and hospitality school in Madrid and started getting the best grades I ever had. I never looked back.

SUDDENLY A LEADER

You realize things when you look back on them. I was always dedicated, curious, humble, responsible, idealistic and patient. I became a leader and a businessman without even realizing it by the sheer force of events. At first I was too young to be the boss, until suddenly one day I was too old to be anything else. I have always tried to set the tone for my team by, for example, being the first one into work.

RESOLVED WITH A HANDSHAKE

My spirit is combative and resistant. I think you can always improve, but sometimes my passion gets the best of me. I have made more than one person cry during an argument, but then I always took the time to explain to them that the search for perfection is separate from them as a person. Everything was resolved with a handshake. Ultimately, as a leader you must be rigorous in the work and demanding of your team, all the while maintaining a sense of humility, curiosity and perseverance.

WHAT IS CREATIVITY?

It's very complicated to define exactly what creativity is. At its core, it is nonconformity. I believe that creativity in the culinary world is tied to knowledge, lack of knowledge, curiosity, discipline, risk, anarchy, a sense of aesthetics and a developed palate.

LET THE 99 GO

Inspiration could come from anywhere. Picasso once said that inspiration will find you while working, but I believe it can also find you while sleeping. There are no rules to how one gets inspired. But he was right: regardless, you need to work. And

you need to know that out of 100 experiments, if only one comes out perfect, that is the definition of success. You need to learn to let go of the other 99 experiments.

THE STARTING POINT

When creating a new dish, sometimes you start with the product. For example, the season for a specific ingredient begins and we want to prepare a recipe we have never tried before with this particular product. Other times the starting point can be a technique. Instead of preparing a product using established methods, we explore new and different ways.

BAG OF MEMORIES

We do not follow the trends or the prescriptions of others, but of course, we are influenced by everything around us. Every time we travel we see and learn about other products, taste different foods, and store these experiences in our bag of memories. The inspiration behind other types of cuisine can itself be an inspiration to create. One thing we must always remember is that every dish needs to constantly evolve. You must always evolve your cooking from the known to the unknown.

RELATIVE PERFECTION

What is most perfect, from an aesthetic or academic point of view, is not always the best. That doesn't mean that we should not pursue perfection—we all pursue perfection—but what could be perfect for me is perhaps not so to others, and vice-versa. In essence, perfection is relative.

BACK TO BASICS

As chefs, we need to be honest, rigorous, critical and analytical. There is a lot of confusion regarding this profession, and there is a lot of curiosity to learn more. At the same time, there is a temptation and an anxiousness among chefs to have an image for image sake, or worse, for the sake of money. We need to go back to the basics of the profession, and why we do what we do.

WORDS OF WISDOM

New and aspiring chefs need to honestly ask themselves whether they want to live the way this profession demands that they live. It's not as hard as some claim, for there are much harder professions. It is simply different. Doing something you are passionate about is one thing, but it is different when you simply have no choice. If you pursue this profession because you don't have a choice, that is something others can feel and sense.

Once you make an honest assessment and decision, you should enroll in culinary school, but not to learn everything. You need to learn how to learn.

Only after school when you join the ranks of a kitchen, put your skills to work and learn from everyone around you will you begin to absorb true knowledge. Do not ever think you know all there is to know. You can learn from anyone and everyone, and inspiration can come from where you least expect it. I have been in the kitchen for over 50 years and I want to learn more now than ever before. Ultimately, with hard work, persistence and patience, you can succeed.

Peter Goossens

BORN IN:

Zottegem, Belgium

BASED IN:

Kruishoutem, Belgium

EXPERIENCE:

36 years

SELECT ACCOLADES:

Hof van Cleve | 97.25/100 in La Liste (2019)

Hof van Cleve | 3 Michelin Stars (2019)

Hof van Cleve | No. 63 on the World's 50 Best (2018)

All Photos by Heikki Verdurme

"All of our dishes start with the product in mind and respect for those who are cultivating the product—gardeners, farmers, fishermen, hunters and cheese refiners."

A YOUNG PASSION

Ever since I was little I wanted to become a chef. I've always had a passion for food and restaurants, and I've always been fond of good food. My mother was a great cook at home and I frequently helped her in the kitchen. We ate classical dishes like Flemish stew, Flemish-style asparagus and *vol-au-vent*. My parents always taught me the importance of seasonal and healthy food, and my passion for good cuisine comes from them.

PARIS INTERN

My first experiences in a professional kitchen were very tough and challenging. It was not easy for an inexperienced Belgian boy to have an internship in Paris. Ultimately, I stayed and worked for three years at renowned restaurants like Pavillon Elysée, Pré Catelan and Lenôtre. I learned that passion, discipline, perseverance and motivation are the real keys to success in this industry.

THE BUSINESS SIDE

One of the most important lessons I learned is that you need to keep the cost of food balanced. You should always compare one supplier with another, not sticking to a single supplier for a specific product. You must work only with those who will give you the absolute best produce at the best price. From a business lens, cost-effectiveness is critical to success.

NEVER REST ON YOUR LAURELS

This profession demands that you give 300 percent of yourself. The best is never enough. Every day you need to be critical to perform even better. Of course, the more you have achieved and the more recognized you become it is difficult to maintain that level of expectation. There is a lot of stress and pressure on you day after day, but that's also why you must never rest on your laurels. You must stay confident, but you must also keep questioning yourself. Over the years I've learned that the key is to convert critical reviews or failure into positivity. This will help you avoid sleepless nights.

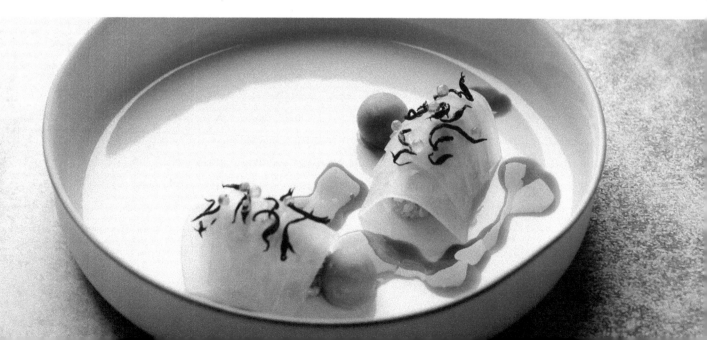

A TRUE CRAFT

All of our dishes in Hof van Cleve start with the product in mind and respect for those who are cultivating the product—gardeners, farmers, growers, fishermen, hunters and cheese refiners. It is from this point of view we create a dish. Out of respect for their passionate work and thanks to their fantastic ingredients, we are able to provide guests with a unique culinary experience. This makes cooking a true craft, and there is no craft without creativity. For us, being creative is intimately tied to a sharp eye for detail, respect for nature and season, and not losing the finesse and tastefulness of cooking.

EXTRA CULINARY PLEASURE

I am mostly inspired by local products. They are a part of the DNA of my kitchen. After all, I love a kitchen with individuality. Local products are a tool here, as I also use products from other countries, especially when they can provide significant added value to my creations. Eastern ingredients, for example, like *yuzu*, *ponzu*, *daidai*, and *sudachi* deserve all the attention because of their unique nature and culinary capabilities. They complement the ensemble, and their subtle nuances and diversity result in extra culinary pleasure.

MIND TO PLATE

When creating a new dish, my starting point is the product. Once I have that product in mind, I start writing out ideas. After we test these ideas in the kitchen, we focus on taste. It must be perfect. Then we focus on the visuals, which should pair with the flavors, textures and other elements of the dish. Finally, the creation process ends with choosing the right vessel or plate to present the dish.

A TEAM EFFORT

Welcoming guests is a pleasure and a privilege. My mission is complete when I see guests leaving Hof van Cleve with big smiles on their faces. This, of course, is due to a team effort—not only the kitchen team, but also the hospitality team led by my wife and lady of the house Lieve. I've learned that you can be the greatest chef in the world but without your team, you are nothing.

Ricardo Costa

BORN IN:

Aveiro, Portugal

BASED IN:

Porto, Portugal

EXPERIENCE:

18 years

SELECT ACCOLADES:

The Yeatman | 90.25/100 in La Liste (2019)

The Yeatman | 2 Michelin Stars (2019)

All Photos Courtesy of The Yeatman

> **"Our dishes aim to transmit the quality and authenticity of Portuguese gastronomy—of our seafood and vegetables—while respecting the seasonality and proximity of their origins."**

A NATURAL PROGRESSION

During the summer holidays when I was very young, I used to keep myself busy working in a restaurant called the Cozinha do Rei, or the King's Kitchen. I began by washing up and helping with basic tasks. When I decided to pursue cooking as a profession, I joined the Hotel School of Coimbra, where I also worked as a trainee and began to take on more responsibility. It was during this time that my passion for cooking really began to grow.

As time went on, challenges became bigger and bigger. New environments and experiences motivated me to become more dedicated. All of these steps were part of a process that happened initially due to my own curiosity and then because of a passion for gastronomy.

COD AND COFFEE

I remember some of the lessons my grandmother taught me when I was young that later on, with professional training, I was able to confirm were important to achieving delicious results. The flavors of cod and coffee, for example, always brought back memories of my childhood, and of snacks and meals with my grandparents. Nowadays, I use these two ingredients in my menus, although not together!

FIVE CORE VALUES

My team knows that we have very defined objectives: to match or surpass our guests' expectations, and to provide them with the highest level of excellence, quality and refinement. To do this, there are five core values that I transmit to my team, and which I consider to be fundamental to the healthy running of a kitchen: respect (mutual and of rules), loyalty, solidarity, precision and discipline. To maintain this level of excellence and consistency, we must always be thinking ahead, anticipating, innovating and planning to evolve so we don't get stuck in the present.

up to date with what is happening in the world. For example, we must be very attentive to new trends in gastronomy as well as new techniques and approaches, and this requires a lot of research. The Internet is an important source to overcome this challenge, as is contact with other chefs, participation in gastronomic events and teamwork.

AWAKENING CREATIVITY

The process of creating a new dish involves extensive investigation and experimentation—some dishes require more than others. This process requires leaving your comfort zone in search of new ideas that will surprise and enrich the guest experience. Creating a dish is not something you can achieve in a single attempt. You need to constantly experiment and imagine, which is why I always carry a notebook with me to jot down new ideas. There are a series of factors which can awaken creativity, but I would highlight our larger challenge of reinventing Portuguese gastronomy.

CULINARY AMBASSADOR

My philosophy is to find a balance between tradition, new techniques, flavors and ideas. I always consider the roots of a dish and Portuguese culture. When a person travels to another country, they want to understand the culture and traditions of that country and that's what I aim to do for those who visit Portugal: be an ambassador for Portuguese flavors through my vision. Our dishes aim to transmit the quality and authenticity of Portuguese gastronomy—of our fish, seafood and vegetables—while respecting the seasonality and proximity of their origins.

BEATING EXPECTATIONS

The greatest challenge of all is to match and, if possible, surpass our guests' expectations. We have a responsibility to create impactful, gastronomic experiences and to achieve this we must be constantly

CONSTANT EVOLUTION

Unless the recipe is perfect, I believe that certain dishes need to evolve because the world has evolved. People are different, food habits have changed, and concerns over food nowadays are different from those of the past. The evolution of a dish is something that happens naturally. It may mean changing some of the ingredients or how they are prepared, or it may mean a tweak to how it is presented on the plate, or the result of other factors that evolve the dish in a completely different direction. The key is to be open to change and evolution.

INSTANT INSPIRATION

Sometimes I look at a product like seafood and an idea immediately springs to mind, which then must be deconstructed, tested, debated with my team and ultimately developed into a final dish. For example, we have a blue lobster dish on the menu that originally came to me during a holiday. With the various ingredients and spices I had at the time, I tried a different way of grilling the lobster, and created a new dish in the process. I then developed the dish further upon return to our kitchen.

THE CHALLENGE OF CREATIVITY

Very often a dish that I had initially conceived of does not turn out the way I thought it would. For example, I've been trying to replicate a sardine dish I have in my mind, but it doesn't translate just yet to where I want it to be. I need to dedicate time and work for the idea to be carried perfectly through. This makes the creative process of each dish more of a challenge, and therefore as chefs, we must be persistent and resilient in order to succeed.

BLOWS YOU AWAY

The perfect dish does exist, but it depends on the individual taste of each person and the emotional and sensory baggage they carry, which will then awaken specific sensations in that person—making it perfect for them. The perfect dish is one that blows you away with technique or ingredients, making you stop and think. Our objective is to create the perfect dish. It is an intrinsic daily goal, but reaching that goal requires failure. Failing is part of the experimental process.

WE ARE WHAT WE EAT

Various studies have proven that certain foods can cause illnesses and others can be considered aids in combatting or preventing health issues. These insights will continue to influence the way in which we eat. In addition, we will focus much more on sustainable, healthy cuisine that is nutritionally well-balanced. In Portugal, for example, I believe we will continually improve on traditional food, as has happened in Japan, France, Italy and other places.

Richard Ekkebus

BORN IN:

Vlissingen, The Netherlands

BASED IN:

Hong Kong SAR, China

EXPERIENCE:

35 years

SELECT ACCOLADES:

Amber | 94.25/100 in La Liste (2019)

Amber | 2 Michelin Stars (2019)

Amber | No. 56 on the World's 50 Best (2018)

All Photos Courtesy of Amber

> **"Nature has provided us with an amazing spectrum of ingredients that do not need improvement or transformation. We are simply protecting and showcasing their genius."**

THE MOMENT

I grew up in a restaurateur's environment as my grandparents had a hotel, café and restaurant. My grandmother looked after the kitchen and my grandfather tended bar. I was in a family business where everyone needed to chip in. I always found myself in the kitchen with my grandmother. I loved to help and even the most tedious jobs like peeling grey shrimp were fun at the time, possibly because my future desire to become a chef was inborn. However, when coming to the critical point where I needed to choose a vocation as a young kid, it never crossed my mind to become a chef. Only later on, when I was a student, did I have a weekend job helping out in a kitchen doing dishes and as a kitchen porter. At that moment, I knew.

A CULINARY JOURNEY

I began my first apprenticeship under Michelin-starred chefs Hans Snijders and Robert Kranenborg. I was fortunate to be awarded "Young Chef of the Year" in Holland, which encouraged me to further perfect my art under the tutelage of some of the greatest three Michelin star chefs in France including Pierre Gagnaire, Alain Passard and Guy Savoy. The latter led me to take up the Executive Chef position at the Royal Palm in Mauritius. It was there that the heavy mix of French, Creole, Dutch and Indian heritage of Mauritian cuisine gave my creative imagination free reign.

After seven years, I moved to The Sandy Lane in Barbados, where the wide-ranging culinary traditions of the Caribbean further seduced me. Finally,

I was attracted to The Landmark Mandarin Oriental, Hong Kong and was pleased to come on board prior to the opening.

THE COLLECTIVE

When you're a young chef, you think it's all about you, your vision, and your techniques. Over time, it becomes evident that it's about the team, and that the strength of the team is in the collective. So mentorship is important, sharing is important, creating an environment where people want to contribute, celebrate success and are allowed to make mistakes is important.

CANNOT PLEASE EVERYONE

There is nothing as subjective as taste. Having said that, we will do everything we can to please each of our guests. After all, we are in the hospitality business. We take constructive comments at heart and will always consider what people offer us as feedback, but at the end of the day, we decide what will help us move forward and improve. Social media has certainly complicated our world as everyone seems to be an expert, but you grow thick skin. After 35 years of cooking, I understand that I can't please everyone.

THE ENEMY OF CREATIVITY

There is no formula to be creative. First, you must be true to yourself. At this age, it's easy for many of us to lose ourselves and head in a direction that may not necessarily reflect who we are as individuals. You need to remind yourself of who you are and what you value, then share it with others. You must also learn to trust your impulses and take risks. Conforming to what everyone else is doing is the biggest enemy of creativity.

THE OLD FASHIONED WAY

You cannot be successful and creative if you stay in one place with blinders on, so traveling is not only an inspiration, but it also gives you energy, resources the brain, rests your body from bone-breaking 16-hour work days, and brings you closer to your loved ones. If I didn't travel, I would probably go mad in this high-energy city. Whether traveling or not, I always have a little notebook with me. Inspiration is plentiful and I write it all down the old fashioned way. Some ideas I use immediately while others sit in the memory bank for months or even years.

MIND TO PLATE

We start with the season, curating a list of products we want to work with. Sometimes there are old time favorites like fresh bamboo shoots in the winter or garden peas in the summer, but sometimes they are ingredients most other chefs ignore. We then work on a concept of a dish that I write in my notebook: the message we want to convey and the flavor profile we're looking for. Most of the time, the initial concept works.

I am 51 years old and my brain is a memory drive of flavors, so the connections between ingredients, tastes and textures come from many years of experience. Then my team starts to work on the individual components and we bring it together. This is at times a rapid process and at times a painstaking one. When we are getting close to a finished product, we involve the sommelier to taste the dish from a wine pairing perspective, for we are a very wine-driven restaurant.

THE GENIUS OF NATURE

We juggle between tradition and modernity on a daily basis. There is no future without the past, and we use a lot of traditional methods. I was trained in French kitchens founded on craftsmanship, the finest ingredients and personality. These ingredients are still part of cooking. Technology has offered us ways to do things better and adopt new techniques should they suit our philosophy, but having said that, we are not an avant-garde restaurant and technique is never more important than the taste. Nature has provided us with an amazing spectrum of ingredients that do not need improvement or transformation. We are simply protecting and showcasing their genius.

NOT A MUSEUM

We love to create dishes and continually perfect them. When we believe there is nothing more to improve—the taste, aroma, presentation, mouth feel and other features, we move on and retire highly successful dishes. The truth is that the repetition we do every day during a particular season, creating a dish over and over again, requires lots of discipline, but it is also a little numbing. We need to change and evolve, and it's our eternal curiosity that continues to be a driving force. We do not rest on our laurels with the classics that we have perfected, for that is not the philosophy at Amber. We are a forward-thinking restaurant and not a museum.

INDUSTRY SHIFTS

Looking ahead, I believe a more social and environmentally-friendlier approach to managing restaurant operations will take hold, favoring smaller, local craftsmen and artisans with a strong focus on the locavore approach. I hope that vegetables become the new proteins, for this is something I have been pushing for the past 12 years. Indeed, beverages too will need to align more with health conscious guests, and there will be a broader demand for interesting non-alcoholic pairings.

Rodolfo Guzmán

BORN IN:

Santiago, Chile

BASED IN:

Santiago, Chile

EXPERIENCE:

20 years

SELECT ACCOLADES:

Boragó | 81.00/100 in La Liste (2019)

Boragó | No. 27 on the World's 50 Best (2018)

Boragó | No. 4 on Latin America's 50 Best (2018)

All Photos Courtesy of Boragó

"Real creativity is an exercise, but it is not for everyone. It can be tiring and disappointing. At the same time, it can be the most comfortable place in the world."

HOW IT ALL STARTED

I grew up splitting my time between the city and the countryside. I would spend the summers with my grandmother while my parents worked in Santiago. When we prepared fresh chicken, everything was done in front of me. It was such a natural extension of how we cooked. There we drank *pojarito* yogurt, warm milk right from the cow, and ate wild summer fruits. These experiences and memories have shaped my relationship with food and my culinary philosophy.

I've always felt that cooks were born to be cooks, and after we train, we become professionals. Growing up, I didn't believe for a second that I would become a professional chef. When I was 19 years old, I moved to Charleston, South Carolina. I needed to earn an income so I was hired as a dishwasher at John's Island café. Ultimately, I ended up cooking all the pastry, which tells you I really wanted to learn, grow and create. It was only after I returned to Chile from South Carolina did a friend of mine recommend culinary school. I had never dreamed of becoming a chef, but at that point in my life, it all made sense.

ASK ME ANYTHING

As an apprentice I was so anxious to start cooking and to learn everything I could, but this attitude became troublesome. I remember the chef de cuisine at the time was a young woman who made the mistake of telling me that no question was a silly question, and to ask her anything at any time. I took her up on this offer and began asking questions—small questions, big questions, all questions. After a few months she yelled at me, telling me to never ask her anything ever again. From that point on, I learned by observing.

ESCAPING REALITY

My first experiences in a professional kitchen in Chile were frustrating and disappointing. The first cook book I bought, The French Laundry by Thomas Keller, spoke passionately about unique ingredients, producers, techniques and processes. But in Chile, restaurants were more focused on decorations rather than the actual dish. You would have someone who returned from traveling, copy a restaurant concept from abroad and open it up in

181

Santiago, then sell it shortly after. Every restaurant had a short economic cycle. I couldn't accept this reality. I had a passion for what I was doing and felt like I was going in the wrong direction, to the wrong place, at the wrong time.

Then one day someone asked me if I had heard about what was happening in Spain. I had no idea. They said it was a gastronomic revolution and that there were incredible restaurants everywhere. It was music to my ears. Since I wanted to escape my reality, I decided to leave it behind and adopt another one. I left everything I had in Chile and went to Spain to learn from scratch.

GROWN IN CHILE

What keeps us motivated and enthusiastic as a team is rooted in curiosity. Year after year, out of sheer curiosity, we have been discovering the possibilities of Chilean cuisine by finding very unique ingredients only grown in our country. We are constantly in discovery mode, and it fuels us as a team and as a restaurant.

ALL IN OUR HEADS

Stress and pressure do not exist outside the mind. You cannot touch it, see it or taste it. It has no col-

or. It is simply in our minds. I always remind the men and women on my team to enjoy every second of what we do because the fact is this: the biggest pressure for a cook is to have an empty restaurant, but if you are lucky enough to have a full house for good reason, then you must celebrate this reality and enjoy it. You must not get trapped with unnecessary stress.

A MOMENT IN TIME

One of the challenges we face is dealing with ingredients that are only available for three to four weeks a year—Quisco parasites and sea stars, among others—and only we have the skills to treat and cut them the way we need them. Over the years we have become deeply involved with such ingredients so that we can take better advantage of their flavors when the time is right.

THE CREATIVE PROCESS

The creative process is one of the most complex things to define and explain, mainly because it is a very personal method. The more disciplined you are and the more structure you have, the more you understand what you've done in the past, where you are now, and where you want to be in the future.

Real creativity is an exercise, but it is not for everyone. It can be tiring and disappointing. At the same time, it can be the most comfortable place in the world. When your cooking style is attached to creativity, then you feel no attachment to what you do. In our case, we are always ready to move forward and focus entirely on learning and discovering new possibilities and combinations of flavors. During this process, inspiration can come from anywhere,

and anything could be a starting point: a product, method, landscape, moment, season or feeling.

AN EMPTY RESTAURANT

At the beginning of the restaurant we had very little attention on the food, hospitality, service, or the discovery of native ingredients. For the first six years, the restaurant was empty. Chileans did not even know we existed, mainly because we were never written about and were full of criticism that tried to discredit our approach, cuisine and philosophy. Fortunately, we've been able to grow, survive and be recognized.

MIND TO PLATE

I always try to draw my thoughts and ideas into my notebooks, categorizing and classifying as I go along. That way the moment I pull them out and cook that recipe for the first time, I have a clear idea of what I wanted to do and how I wanted to do it. Sometimes those ideas become a dish in a week or less, and other times it may take months or even years. There have also been many times where we revive dishes from ten years ago with a new twist on flavor, ingredients or technique. To me, creating a dish is a permanent exercise in progress.

24 HOURS TO 3 YEARS

On one occasion I wanted to create a new dish over the summer that was very fresh, raw, floral and aromatic using giant squid. I started drawing the dish in a very Japanese-style execution, where you couldn't see anything but two ingredients on top: aloe vera and squid. Everything else was hiding inside the symmetrical cuts. We plated that exact drawing within a day, and it was on the menu within 24 hours. On the other hand, we have a dessert called The Black Sheep of the Family. It took us three years to reach a point where it was ready to be put on the menu.

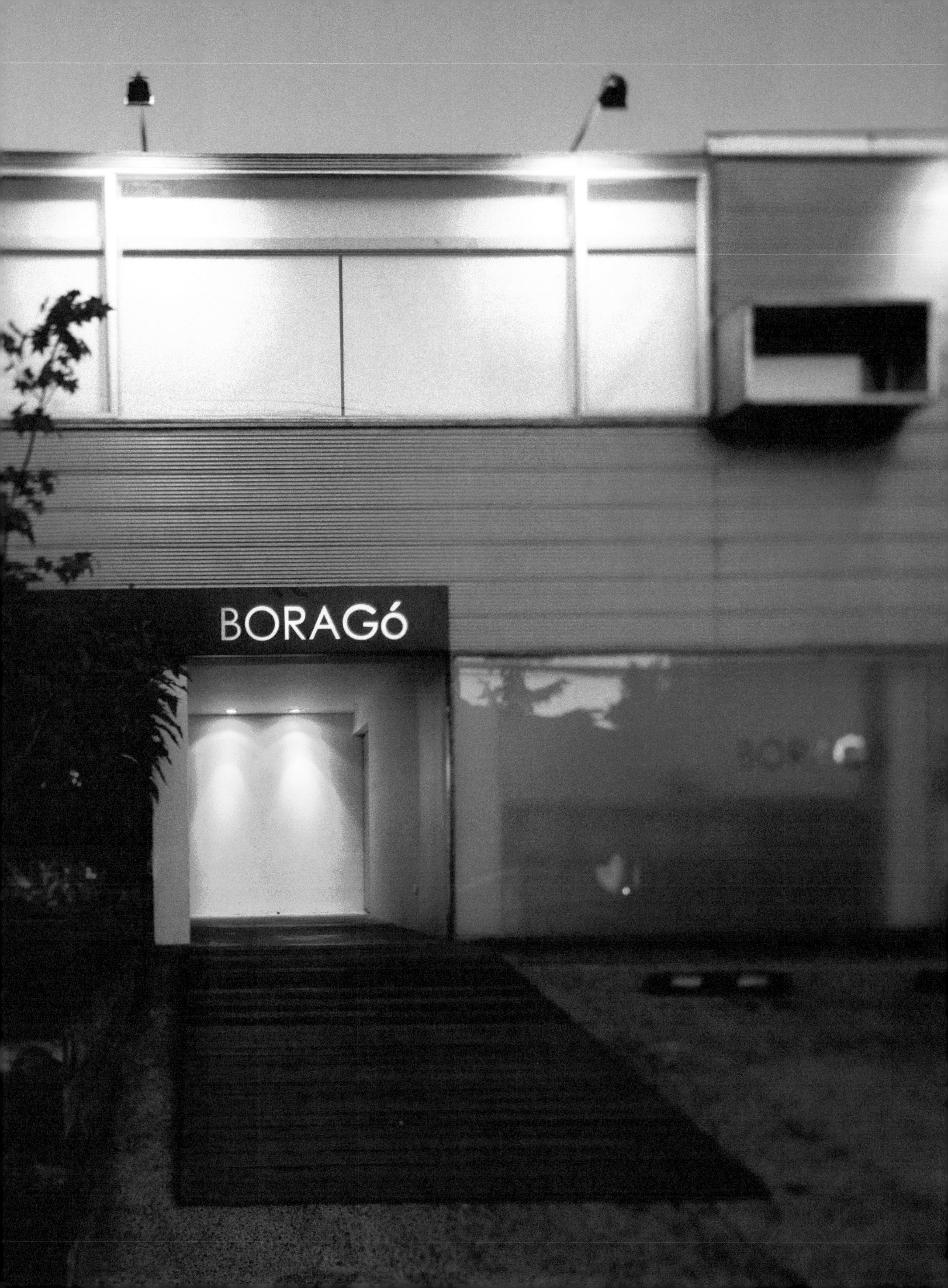
BORAGó

Ryuki Kawasaki

BORN IN:

Niigata, Japan

BASED IN:

Bangkok, Thailand

EXPERIENCE:

21 years

SELECT ACCOLADES:

Mezzaluna | 91.50/100 in La Liste (2019)

Mezzaluna | 2 Michelin Stars (2019)

> **"Every dish has a lifecycle and we need to continually reinvent our menu. We need to change with the times."**

A NATURAL INTEREST

When I was young I loved to help my mother and grandmother in the kitchen. It was this natural interest that propelled me to pursue this profession. After high school I joined the Tsuji Culinary Institute in Tokyo. My first experiences in a professional kitchen were challenging, but I was just happy to be in the kitchen. I knew that challenges were necessary to grow both personally and professionally, and I consider every challenge to be a learning opportunity.

ROOTED IN RESPECT

When I was a junior in this industry I looked to my seniors for inspiration and observed closely how they managed a big team. Reflecting on these issues, the most important aspects of leadership are communication with your team and listening to your diners. Everything is rooted in respect. I also believe that a leader must coach and motivate their team to excellence.

MOLDING THE TEAM

One of the biggest challenges to leading a restaurant is managing the staff. We need to train the team, work as a team and trust the team. This is easier said than done as people come with different qualifications, backgrounds, years of experience and environments that are different than ours. Upgrading the skillset of colleagues is another key challenge as there is constant change in the world of food, and we need a team that is always aware of the latest developments, techniques and methods.

BRIDGING PAST AND PRESENT

When creating a new dish, the food must be seasonal and tasty. Therefore, it is important to have a solid understanding of the marketplace and the availability of ingredients. It's also important to understand our roots and the origin of many of our traditional ways of cooking. Today, we must also incorporate modern methods, techniques and ideas. In the end, what goes on the plate is as important as the way in which it is presented.

LEARNING FROM THE BEST

My experiences working with Michelin-starred chefs was my "a-ha" moment. Their dedication, hard work, eye for detail and pursuit of perfection were some of the things that I observed working in France, Japan and the United States.

My inspiration comes from using seasonal products and infusing them with both Japanese and French culture. For example, we serve the Niigata

Murakami Wagyu Beef A5 at Mezzaluna. It is grilled over *binchotan* charcoal, and is a perfect example of what I call a Japanese touch to a French dish. While the beef and charcoal are sourced from Japan, the way in which it is cooked and presented is French, and that's the twist.

CHANGING WITH THE TIMES

The perfect dish may exist, but not forever, for there is a timespan for everything in life. We need to keep evolving and I am of the position that cooking changes with the times. We cannot be rigid with our menu. The availability of seasonal products guides everything we do, and that itself is what change is all about. Every dish has a lifecycle and we need to keep reinventing our menu before our diners get tired.

MIND TO PLATE

When creating a new dish I first research products that are in season. Once I make a decision on the products I want to work with, I think about the best ways in which we can cook them, serve them, and with which flavor combinations and profiles will they work best. The dish in question must also be integrated into the balance and flow of the overall menu, so there are lots of considerations to keep in mind. Once created, I write the recipe down and have a discussion with my team. After trial, error, and improvements over multiple tastings, including how we present the dish, we settle on what we believe is the perfect dish. When ready, we train both the kitchen and staff in our latest creation.

MAKE YOUR MARK

For new and aspiring chefs, I would advise you to thoroughly learn the basics before longing for anything fancy. You must be ready to challenge everything. Being a chef is a tough job and you should be prepared to work long hours. No one can become an expert chef overnight. It takes years of learning on the job before you can step out on your own and make your mark.

Sean
Gray

BORN IN:

Bucks County, PA, USA

BASED IN:

New York, NY, USA

EXPERIENCE:

16 years

SELECT ACCOLADES:

Ko | 83.00/100 in La Liste (2019)

Ko | 2 Michelin Stars (2019)

Ko | No. 62 on the World's 50 Best (2018)

Photo to the Left by Zack DeZon

> **"Creativity is like a muscle—it needs exercise or it atrophies—and working with a group of creative people helps me build that muscle constantly."**

A BUDDING INTEREST

My earliest memory of wanting to be a chef is from the fourth grade. My teacher assigned us professions and we had to interview someone who did that job. I was given a chef and my interest developed from there. In middle school, I had a great home economics teacher who could tell that I was interested in food. She encouraged me to go to culinary school and signed me up for the Culinary Institute of America mailing list. I was eager to learn more and I'm glad that I was encouraged to follow that path.

SMALL VICTORIES

When I first joined a professional kitchen I loved it immediately. I joke that kitchens back then were homes for lost souls. I had an instant connection with those around me. For many of us cooking, it felt like the only job we were suited for. I liked the repetitiveness of the work. Even as a young cook, you're solving problems all day. There were lots of small victories and rewards along the way that made it enticing for me. It's hard when you're starting out, but time helps with that. Working and growing helped me learn to trust my instincts.

PURSUIT OF PERFECTION

When cooking fish for a tasting menu, you have a similar menu every day with the same fish. Your portion size is almost always the same and your cooking technique is almost always the same. However, the variables that do change are how you season the fish, how hot the pan is, and when you add the butter or additional fats. If you're paying attention to all the small details of that process, you can watch something get better or worse over time. So with each customer, you have this opportunity to perfect each step until you get to the perfect result.

EVOKING AN EMOTION

At Ko, we're not chained to one style of cuisine or one set of ingredients. It's very freeing, but it's also very challenging. With few formal constraints, we still need a starting point for creativity and for us, that's the guest. Part of that is the function of Ko's design: we're cooking directly in front of our diners so we can see their reaction to our work in real time. We have to rely on intuition and emotion to understand what our guests will react to, while staying true to our core philosophy and approach.

A FINE BALANCE

Often times the simplest things are the most refined. This is something that I've learned working with David Chang. But simple doesn't mean rustic. We apply technique to common ingredients with the aim of finding the meeting point of simple and refined. For us at Ko, it means eschewing excess ornamentation and flourishes that aren't rooted in flavor. We are never different for the sake of being different. At the same time, we try not to reference anyone but ourselves. It's a fine balance but if your aim is simplicity and directness, it helps you get closer to creating the right dish.

STRENGTH IN DIVERSITY

We hire for technical ability but we're really looking for people who are a personality fit. Ko's strength comes from the diverse backgrounds of our staff: people who are from a more traditional fine dining rooted in French cuisine, to others who have a stronger Japanese background, to still others who have experience working in Europe. We also have colleagues who have worked in high volume Italian restaurants, and some who have never worked in a professional kitchen before. It's a challenge to help everyone develop their technical skills, but ultimately, people from diverse backgrounds make all of us better because of what they bring.

MIND TO PLATE

One example of a dish that came together serendipitously is the wild rice ice cream dessert, which

Photos to the Left (top to bottom) by Andrew Bezek, Zack DeZon, Andrew Bezek

very much reflects our creative process at Ko. We had been working for a while on an idea of a rice, or rice milk ice cream. We wanted to end the meal with what could be interpreted as a bowl of rice. Through countless versions of recipes of rice ice cream, it never had the right consistency or feeling. After a long process, we came to the conclusion that we needed to find a way to control the variables of the gluten found in rice, which was the biggest problem in getting the right texture. We then started using a long grain wild rice, which we could cook or puff from frying in hot oil.

Completely unrelated to the rice ice cream effort, we had once forgotten about some *kombu*, or kelp, toasting in an oven. It was something that I had brushed with oil and then wanted to lightly toast before adding to a *dashi*, or Japanese stock. What came out was almost caramelized and had a potato chip texture. We thought that this would be something that we could candy using a *dragée* method after breaking the *kombu* into small enough crumbs. This is a technique used to mask something bitter by coating it in something sweet. Here we thought that a kind of dessert *furikake* would be simple, flavorful, and have a sense of originality to it. But alas, we had no use for it, and couldn't seem to work it into any of the other dishes.

Then it hit us, merging the two concepts and components together worked really well, and it finally made sense as a dish.

CREATIVITY IS LIKE A MUSCLE

Creativity is like a muscle—it needs exercise or it atrophies—and working with a group of creative people helps me build that muscle constantly. We're also lucky to have an adjoining bar to our main dining room. The pressure to create something perfect is less there. It's a space for us to try out new ideas that might not be ready for our tasting menu. At the bar we can make dishes that people wouldn't expect from us, which has allowed us to break our conception of what a "Ko dish" is and create even more freely.

WORDS OF WISDOM

Write down everything you can and develop a system to keep track of your ideas and what you're learning. This is incredibly important. It really helps you to see the progression of your ideas and helps you develop your own voice as a chef. Too many cooks just take photos of dishes, but I believe that actually using pen and paper makes the connection in your brain. Finally, to be a chef you just have to start cooking. Of course it's important to set goals for yourself, but don't get hung up on where you're working to start. I am not the product of fine-dining institutions. With the right attitude, you can learn so much from any restaurant. It doesn't have to be the fanciest restaurant.

Photo to the Right by Zack DeZon

Sven Elverfeld

BORN IN:

Hanau, Germany

BASED IN:

Wolfsburg, Germany

EXPERIENCE:

30 years

SELECT ACCOLADES:

Aqua | 98.50 /100 in La Liste (2019)

Aqua | 3 Michelin Stars (2018)

Aqua | No. 73 on the World's 50 Best (2018)

Photos to the Left and Right by Wonge Bergmann

"The order in which you should eat a dish influences the way in which you should plate a dish."

A DISAPPEARING ARTFORM

Since I can remember, I've always wanted to practice a profession that combined craftsmanship with creativity. This led me to complete an apprenticeship as a pastry chef, and then as a chef. My first apprenticeship as a confectioner was in a small, traditional bakery, of which there were many at the time that made their own chocolates and tarts. I was fortunate to be the only apprentice in training for all three years. My superior was quite young himself and he really encouraged me onward. He predicted that craftsmanship in the confectionery sector would disappear more and more and would only be economically viable for a few companies. I heeded his advice and, for me to continue working creatively and artfully, as well as broaden my horizons, I started my second apprenticeship as a chef. I am still very grateful for his advice.

DEVELOPING YOUR TEAM

Above all, the most important leadership insight I've learned is to stay humble and treat every member of your team with respect. One of the biggest challenges to leading a restaurant like Aqua is finding the right staff. Therefore, it is critical to strengthen and improve the skills of the team regularly, offering them new opportunities to grow both personally and professionally. I do this by rotating the responsibility of different stations in the kitchen—*saucier, entremetier, poissonnier*—so everyone has a chance to develop and learn new skills over time. The bottom line is you can't be successful without a passionate team committed to a shared vision.

THE NATURE OF CREATIVITY

In my mind, creativity is an innate ability and cannot be taught. However, creativity itself can be influenced by many different aspects: childhood memories, your home country, travels abroad, special products and more. All these aspects have an influence on my own creativity. For example, we have a few dishes that include Frankfurt's specialty—the green sauce—because this reminds me of my childhood growing up. Green sauce is made of seven different kinds of herbs including borage, chervil, cress, parsley, salad burnet, sorrel and chives, as well as garlic, sour cream, yogurt, mustard, vegetable oil, lemon juice, salt and pepper. Another example is a dish that was inspired from my travels abroad: pigeon breast "Jean Claude Miéral" with eggplant, avocado, soya, pak choi, roasted garlic and bergamot.

MENTALLY FREE

The products of each season are my main inspiration when creating a new dish. However, you cannot force inspiration by telling yourself you need a new idea, or by looking left or right in a panic. Most of my ideas come when I am mentally free and usually when I am not at work. The secret to being inspired is letting your mind wander in an environment unrelated to your daily routine.

MIND TO PLATE

The moment I have an idea I write it down on a piece of paper—wherever I am, wherever I go.

Later, I turn these ideas into mind maps because this helps me organize what's in my head and how I could put it on a plate. I then think about the combination of products and their flavors, textures and cooking techniques including fermenting, simmering, pickling or otherwise. When I have made a decision, I prepare all of the products and think about the order in which you should eat every component. The order in which you should eat the dish influences the way in which you should plate the dish. That's why I always try my dishes before I think about plating.

INTELLIGENT CUISINE

When you examine our dishes, balancing tradition with new techniques, flavors and ideas is omnipresent in our menus. Knowledge of traditional cooking methods and products are essential to creating a modern, intelligent cuisine. I think one example of this is my reconstruction of a classic German dish: simmered corned beef from Müritz lamb with Frankfurt-style green sauce, potato and egg.

Photos to the Left by Wonge Bergmann
Photo to the Right by Götz Wrage

Tetsuya Wakuda

BORN IN:

Hamamatsu, Shizuoka Prefecture, Japan

BASED IN:

Singapore

EXPERIENCE:

36 years

SELECT ACCOLADES:

Waku Ghin | 88.50/100 in La Liste (2019)

Waku Ghin | No. 23 on Asia's 50 Best (2019)

Waku Ghin | 2 Michelin Stars (2018)

Photo to the Left Courtesy of Marina Bay Sands

"I thrive on being able to serve my guests something I've created from inspiration to table."

TEACH ME EVERYTHING

I moved to Australia at the age of 22 and started as a kitchen-hand in a restaurant in Sydney. At the time, I had no language skills, no cooking skills, and no knowledge of food or techniques, but I was very curious and keen to learn. This was the beginning of my journey. I remember being in this big, beautiful kitchen of legendary chef Tony Bilson. He showed me what he did and I was fascinated. He was an enormous influence on me and I learned a lot about French cuisine.

OUR LOVE OF FOOD

Running a restaurant is not a solo effort. Everyone on the team contributes to make it work. All of us have come from different backgrounds, studied different methods and grown up in different environments. Despite these differences, all of us are aligned in our love of food, and all of us desire to bring the best possible dining experience we can to our guests. I believe that when everyone is clear on their responsibilities and our common goals, and they perform their best, we can achieve greatness.

CORE PHILOSOPHY

The act of cooking is a gift from the chef to the diner. This philosophy remains constant regardless of any awards or recognition we may receive. Every single day at Waku Ghin, we continue to do what we believe in, which is to source the best possible ingredients from around the world and deliver them to guests with the highest standards of service.

JOINING A VILLAGE

At Tetsuya's in Sydney, almost everything was under my control—the building, the business and the sourcing. In not so many words, I was in charge. But when I opened Waku Ghin at Marina Bay Sands in Singapore, it was a very different experience as it was like joining a village. We are a community of restaurants and I had to learn to build relationships with management, fellow chefs and their restaurant teams. Having run Tetsuya's on my own for decades, I had to start learning from scratch about how to operate a restaurant in a large-scale, integrated resort.

I BEGIN TO WONDER

Creativity is rooted in curiosity. From the very beginning of the culinary process, when we start sourcing ingredients, creativity is a driving force. When I travel and visit restaurants, I pay close attention to the ingredients they use. And every time I experience something interesting—for example, a great flavor or scent—I begin to wonder. How do I incorporate this into my menu? What type of dish can I make using this ingredient? Different cuisines and cultures open up our minds and sharpen our insights about the endless possibilities in the kitchen.

THE TENDER SPOT

Ingredients are at the center of all my creations. When I am inspired to create a new dish, it usually starts with an ingredient that I personally enjoy. Once we have that ingredient, we try to elevate it with simple flavors that enhance the texture and taste—nothing too complicated that takes away the focus.

For example, Tasmanian ocean trout is fantastic. Grilled or oven-baked, the taste and texture come together perfectly. The sides and surfaces would be fully cooked, but the pinkish portion in the middle—the tender spot—always tasted the best. This is what sparked the creation of the Ocean Trout Confit served at Tetsuya's. I wanted to replicate that same tenderness in the middle throughout the whole dish.

Photos to the Left (top to bottom): Courtesy of Tetsuya, Courtesy of Marina Bay Sands, Courtesy of Tetsuya

PURSUIT OF PERFECTION

As chefs, we always aim for perfection, but there is no such thing as a perfect dish in this world. Everyone has different preferences and taste buds, and that is what makes working in this industry so interesting. It's a constant process of change, evolution, and refinement. Setbacks are not the result of creative failure. They are opportunities to improve and tweak, and to make the dining experience better for our guests.

Photo Above Courtesy of Marina Bay Sands
Photo to the Right Courtesy of Tetsuya

THE PERFECT MEAL

More than 20 years ago I dined at an eight-seat restaurant named Kahala in Osaka, Japan, and this dining experience was the closest to what I would describe as a perfect meal. It was an amazing experience unlike any other. The creativity, taste, and precision in the culinary craft hit just the right spot for a truly memorable experience that I still cherish today.

THE SIMPLER THE BETTER

In the future, I believe simple dishes will take the hearts of diners. There will be less complicated methods and less garnish without sacrificing taste. While there is a growing appreciation for premium ingredients, diners still prefer to taste ingredients in all their naturalness and without much embellishment. Over the years, I've learned that great cuisine comes not from elaborate cooking but from fresh ingredients and unadorned techniques. This idea also aligns with our aging society. Everyone is more health-conscious and prefers gentler flavors.

SHARED EARTH

Sustainability is at the top our list as chefs. It's about maintaining a natural balance between enjoying the gifts of nature and giving back to the environment. Even as we source fresh, natural produce for our cuisine, we want to do it in a way that protects the natural ecosystem so that it continues to thrive. In Australia and New Zealand, most seafood are farmed to minimize the threat of overfishing to the natural marine ecosystem. There is also a cap quota for the farming and supply of ingredients like scampi and crayfish.

Many years ago, I started the Petuna Ocean Trout breeding program in Tasmania to educate people to produce ocean trout in an ethically-responsible way. Among its many sustainability measures, Petuna produces ocean trout at a low pen density, so that they have room to move and are therefore healthy and stress-free. Today, Ocean Trout Confit is one of our signature dishes at Tetsuya's in Sydney.

MORE SEAFOOD, LESS MEAT

In Singapore, Waku Ghin sources from the best and most environmentally-friendly suppliers, and focuses on less resource-intensive sources of protein—favoring premium seafood over animal husbandry. Our *hojicha*, or Japanese green tea, is sourced from a certified supplier from Kyoto, and the restaurant's seaweed is naturally harvested as well.

THE WHOLE EXPERIENCE

Having a career in the culinary industry requires more than simply knowing how to cook. We must have deep knowledge of beverages and service, too. People eat for the experience, so we must consider the whole experience when we look for inspiration and how best to improve our craft. It's also important to track the evolving taste buds of guests, and keep an eye out for new taste profiles and ingredients that can be further explored and enhanced. If you're in this industry, you must love to eat, to taste, and to experiment, and you must retain this natural curiosity to continually improve.

Photo to the Right Courtesy of Marina Bay Sands

Virgilio Martínez

BORN IN:

Lima, Peru

BASED IN:

Lima, Peru

EXPERIENCE:

20 years

SELECT ACCOLADES:

Central | 94.50/100 in La Liste (2019)

Central | No. 6 on the World's 50 Best (2018)

Central | No. 2 on Latin America's 50 Best (2018)

All Photos by César del Rio

> **"Once we decided to base our dishes on altitude, with ingredients found together in the same regions, the menu practically wrote itself."**

A SEED WAS PLANTED

My father would take me to very good restaurants all over Peru and other capitals of gastronomy around the world so I developed an appreciation and understanding of fine dining at a very young age. These early experiences planted a seed of interest, curiosity and marvel about the world of cooking and restaurants.

MY FIRST CHOICE

I always wanted to be a professional skateboarder. Place to place, street to street, it was amazing to explore Lima by skateboard. We live in a multicultural city and I was always meeting and connecting with different people. It's my nature. I've always been a skater, and that requires focus, precision, passion and a willingness to go to the extreme to reach your goals. Most of my friends, too, are creative, sporty, committed and extreme in their own way. We feed off each other and we support each other.

ORGANIZED CHAOS

Before stepping foot in a kitchen more than 20 years ago, I had absolutely no idea how a kitchen was run. It was completely unknown to me. So when I witnessed chefs at work for the first time, they were incredibly passionate, working together towards the same goal amidst a kind of chaos. But of course, it was not chaos. It was a well-oiled machine. I saw my own life in that contradiction. Being in a kitchen was like a performance filled with art, passion, technique and structure. I was hooked.

FAILING MORE THAN BEFORE

In the past, I cared a lot about criticism and critical reviews. Today, it is much less so. The main person who can criticize me is myself. When I push myself to deeper self-reflection, I think about what is good and fair for my team. That is what I care about most. And as we get more and more adventurous exploring new territories and ingredients, I fail more now than I did before. When you compete with yourself, this is not a sign of mediocrity. It is a sign of learning and progress.

CULTURE OF COLLABORATION

When we ask people to work with us, we are looking for kind, committed, passionate and detail-oriented people with personality and emotion.

The time we spend together in the kitchen and in conversation is very important, and we treat each other as family. I think one of the reasons people are motivated to join our team is because I want to integrate different disciplines into the gastronomic experience. I can only do this by creating a culture of collaboration, and by empowering every individual to contribute their own ideas and experiences to help shape our collective effort.

THE MEASURE OF SUCCESS

When people say you're successful, they are projecting their definition of success onto you from afar. They ascribe to you accomplishment, happiness and joy. But that doesn't make it true. You could be successful in their eyes but unhappy at heart. So how does one understand and measure success? For me, family, community, working together, good relationships and a sense of responsibility and gratitude all play an important role in my definition.

Success, however, is a daily pursuit: you have to work each and every day to reach your goals. I don't think I'm better than the next chef because I received some award. If you only focus on accolades and awards, your ego will drive your life. I don't think this is healthy nor wise. I think we should be critical of ourselves, our behaviors, motivations and decisions. It's not all about gastronomy. It's about life, connection, community, friendship and family.

GOOD MORNING

I wake up in a creative mode: sensitive, positive, open to possibilities, and energized to move, cook and connect with others. Peru is a place where you

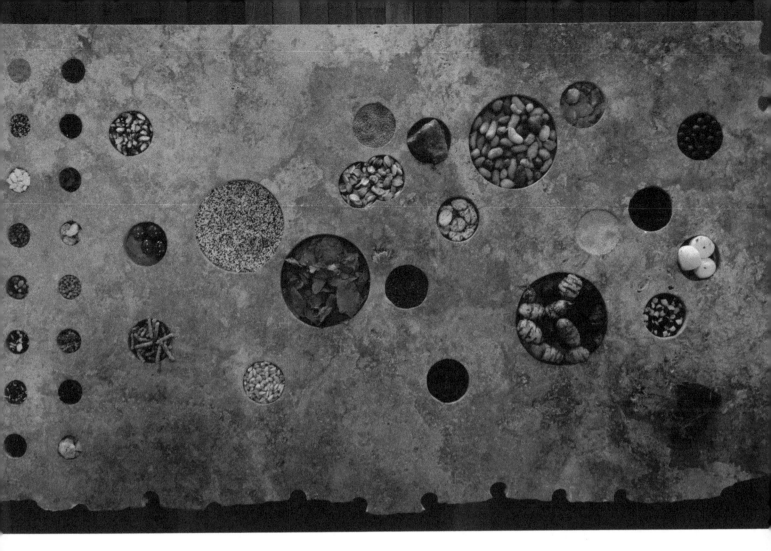

can find inspiration everywhere. Creativity sparks from exploration, traveling, meeting people and asking questions you don't normally ask. We regularly change our menu due to seasonality, altitude and because we feel we have to: new ingredients and new inspirations encourage us to constantly experiment.

THE FULL PICTURE

At Central we cook ecosystems. The plate has to communicate what we experience in nature. When we think about the ingredients that make up a dish, we are thinking about the entire dish. No single ingredient is prized more than another. Each is as integral to the recipe as it is to its own ecosystem.

REDISCOVERING THE ROOTS

We've chosen to renounce all products and textures not found naturally in Peru—common things that have become standard cooking tools among restaurants worldwide like fancy powders, industrial sweeteners, magic thickeners, and untraceable oils. We replace them with ingredients found within our environment in Peru. This is our proudest achievement at Central. It has been a long, gradual process that has repeatedly challenged and pushed us in new directions we never thought were possible. In time, we realized that we already have everything we need.

In Puno, on the vast, treeless plateau, quinoa powder is used as a thickener in soups. In Puerto Mal-

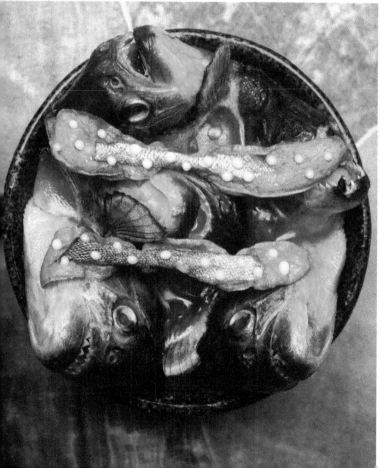

donado, in the jungle, macerated fruits are used to sweeten. A high-jungle cactus called *airampo* and cochineal insects could be used as colorants. It dawned on us: if we are so rich with resources, why do we have to import unnecessary ingredients from elsewhere?

INSPIRED BY THE WILD

When creating a new dish, the first thing we do is plan a trip. With little knowledge of what we're about to discover or with whom we're going to meet when we get there, we fly to different regions of Peru with our research team from Mater Iniciativa. After our adventure, we take our ideas to the kitchen. We think back and discuss all the ingredients we discovered in the wilderness, and we just start cooking. It's a very organic process of creation. Balancing tradition with new ingredients, techniques, flavors and ideas is a powerful learning process, and in that sense, we must never be afraid to fail in an effort to create something extraordinary. Indeed, failure is the only path to such an achievement.

MIND TO PLATE

As we looked at all the variables of Peru's ecosystems, altitude kept appearing over and over again. Peru's topography is uneven, which may sound chaotic or unwelcoming, and yet it is anything but. Once we decided to base our dishes on altitude, with ingredients found together in the same regions, the menu practically wrote itself. It was risky because we were getting into something that was conceptual, but we couldn't sit still. We had to work hard to make these obscure ingredients— things like *chaco clay* or *maca root*—seem as familiar in the restaurant as they were in their own ecosystem. Instead of shaving truffles, we shave *tunta*, a freeze-dried potato.

THE PERFECT MOMENT

I don't think the perfect dish exists because perfection calls for obsession, which has a negative feeling. I do, however, believe in the perfect moment. It could last a few seconds or a few minutes, but it doesn't happen on a regular basis. Characterized by happiness and beauty, the perfect moment requires great food, company, atmosphere, location and many other factors that are hard to predict or plan, so you should simply let things happen naturally.